MW00489611

Stoicism and the Statehouse

STOICISM
AND THE
STATEHOUSE

An Old Philosophy Serving a New Idea

PAT MCGEEHAN

WYTHE-NORTH
PUBLISHING

©2017 Pat McGeehan. All rights reserved.

Wythe-North Publishing

No part of this book may be reproduced
in any form or by any means, electronic or mechanical,
including photocopying, recording, or by any information
storage and retrieval system, without permission
in writing from the publisher.

Front cover image: *Cicero Denounces Catiline*, Cesare Maccari, 1888.

Back cover image: *Cato of Utica Reading the "Phaedo" before
Committing Himself to Death*, Jean-Baptiste Roman and Francois Rude, 1832.

Printed in the United States of America

Library of Congress Control Number: 2017942677

ISBN-13: 978-0-9907386-1-9 (Softcover)

Wythe-North Publishing
P.O. Box 1208
Proctorville, Ohio 45669-1208
www.wythe-north.com

Rather fail with honor than succeed by fraud.

— *Sophocles*

Table of Contents

Acknowledgments vii

Foreword ix

Preface xv

Introduction. xxv

Part I: Stoicism. 1

Chronology 13

Part II: Cato the Younger 21

Part III: Stoic Counsel 95

Know what you can control and what you can't 97

Be comfortable by yourself. 99

You must forego power. 100

Introduce your own ideas, irrespective of the result 101

Others will scorn you. 102

Avoid making deals 103

Don't participate in trivial pleasures 105

Self-restraint requires practice. 107

Correctly judge your observations 109

Resist personal ambition. 111

Ignore the chatter from others 113

Concentrate on your main duty 115

Speak the truth. 116

Victory will be rare. 118

Endure the consequences 120

Mental strength takes work 122

Practicing morality is better than proving it 123

Build courage. 125

Insults are to be taken, not given 127

Familiarize yourself with nonconformity 128

Appendices. 129

Recommended Reading on Stoicism 131

Suggested Reading: Free Markets & Non-Intervention. . . . 132

Bibliography. 136

About the Author. 152

Acknowledgments

This book is dedicated to those who keenly pursue the truth, undeterred by the many who settle for less. Once found, intellectual honesty must be practiced. Sincere men will live it. Otherwise the truth was never sought, but merely the outward prospects from its superficial chase. Ignorance can easily be forgiven though, for fools cannot look past their own oblivion. In the case of men who discover truth, yet shun its exercise—pardon should not be so swift.

I am especially grateful to James Aragon, who not only wrote a very humbling foreword, but is a loyal friend of truth and has always encouraged my devotion to the same. A special mention goes to Chris Calton for reliably editing my work and providing several helpful suggestions. Most of all, I hold in heart my daughter Kennedy—that she may realize a peaceful future of free will and free mind. Only the Lord can know how much I love her.

As a lifelong Catholic and a Sunday school teacher at my local parish, some may find fault with my practice of the Stoic philosophy. Others may even claim the two cannot be reconciled.

Apart from the influence of Stoic ethics on early Christian thought, criticism of this sort will never cease to be heaped from the 'mystics'—as it once was so bitterly levied against the greatest of Christ's theologians, Saint Thomas Aquinas.

Harmonizing the Gospel with the pagan philosophy of Aristotle, St. Thomas imparted profound wisdom, opening the door to invite the rest of Western civilization. Between my faith and philosophy, I find no conflict. But words from this revolutionary saint will serve as my answer to the unconscious Platonic disciples and Manicheans of the present age: 'Reason in man is rather like God in the world.'

Foreword

Pat McGeehan was just a teenager, years away from joining the Air Force, when he tragically lost his father, Lieutenant Colonel Mark McGeehan. Commanding officers ignored the pleas from Pat's dad to ground a reckless senior pilot. After his requests fell on deaf ears, Colonel McGeehan issued a standing order to his own men: they were never to fly with this rogue officer. Instead, Colonel McGeehan placed himself in harm's way. If anyone had to fly with this dangerous wild card, Mark McGeehan would. He was true to his word.

Standing near the flight line, a youthful Pat McGeehan witnessed his father's traumatic demise, when the rogue officer crashed and exploded the B-52 bomber Colonel McGeehan had volunteered to co-pilot, to ensure none of his subordinate airmen were on board. Mark McGeehan's heroic plight made me realize that there are great leaders in uniform, but the uniform also finds itself on plenty who lack character.

Pat and I would not meet until well after the catastrophe at Fairchild AFB that took his father's life. In 1996, as a very junior enlisted military intelligence analyst, my trust in Air Force leadership was permanently diminished when I learned the details behind his father's death through national headlines. But a decade after that fatal disaster, my own emotional response to meeting Mark McGeehan's son and our joint reflection on the tragedy forever bound us.

I have now known Pat McGeehan for thirteen years, and his journey to adopting the Stoic philosophy is a story to be written. When I served under Pat in 2004, he was a brash, young commissioned officer fresh out of intelligence training. I was an arrogant non-commissioned officer with about eight years of experience on him. We hit it off right away. We were both high-achievers with disdain for those incapable of carrying their own weight and an understanding that 'the brass' was often guilty of such ineptitude.

In 2005, we were deployed to the Middle East together. I was an intelligence collection manager; he was Chief Analyst for the Afghanistan Desk. The job of Chief Afghanistan Analyst for the Air Operations Center was sort of a joke. Hundreds of analysts throughout the intelligence community were working on the Afghanistan problem set. With no meaningful air threat, Pat's assignment was more ceremonial than functional. We worked separate shifts, so he would religiously wake me in the middle of my sleep cycle for 120-degree outings to the cigar shed. I didn't smoke, but I enjoyed our chats. We shared a love of domestic politics, foreign policy, and our profession of intelligence.

It would be almost another ten years before Pat would seek to master his emotions, but his Stoic humility was evident very early in our relationship. While the commanding officer wanted him to focus on the mundane task of regurgitating the collective consensus of the intelligence community, Pat had other ideas. He educated himself on Afghanistan. He read about the experiences of the Soviet Union, the British Empire, even Alexander the Great. Pat discovered a pattern through each of these historical occupations that correlated with current events. He conveyed this to his superiors, who casually reiterated that they just wanted 'news reporting.' So Pat quietly wrote up a simple, two-page executive summary explaining why the US Army should establish a forward operating base in a certain eastern province to thwart what he foresaw as a coming offensive by the Taliban. He pushed his report to any analytical desk he could find—and then waited.

In the meantime, Pat withstood severe ridicule. Several high-ranking officers belittled his report, laughing at his appraisal and claiming his anticipated prognosis to be impossible. Some even went so far as to attack him personally. But he calmly held his ground and never backed off his assessment.

As it turned out, Pat's prediction was right, and so was his advice. In fact, his recommendation was acted upon. A couple months later, the Army moved a defensive base to this region, which was met by surging attacks from the Taliban in their attempt to control the battlespace. We both exalted his achievement, but Pat took the humble route and never tried to ingratiate himself with leadership. He simply did what the taxpayer was paying him to do.

Over the next few years, Pat would face incredible personal struggles. His marriage dissolved, he requested early separation from the military, and he set out to be an entrepreneur in his hometown. His endeavor was successful out of the gate, but as with many new ventures, timing was paramount. The financial crisis of 2008 and its ensuing market collapse brought about the unraveling of Pat's business.

After I returned later that year from another overseas tour of duty, we caught up. I had discovered the ideas of liberty through Dr. Ron Paul's candidacy for the Republican Presidential nomination, but Pat had aligned himself with John McCain. At the time, Pat was also campaigning to become the first Republican state representative to be elected from his West Virginia district in more than fifty years. Naturally, we had conversations about war, role of government, and principle.

One fateful day, a conversation about the faults of Abraham Lincoln, a President he adored, nearly threatened our friendship. But Pat is unafraid to examine new ideas, so I suggested he read *The Real Lincoln* by Thomas DiLorenzo. This was the first domino to fall toward Pat's rejection of statism. He then devoured books on liberty, economics, and philosophy, and he became a supporter of Ron Paul's campaign. He went on to publish his first book, *Printing Our Way to Poverty*—a far-reaching exposition about American monetary policy and the damaging results of inflationary economics.

Pat also found success in his first election to the state legislature, making headlines in his own right. But he did not curry favor with his Republican Party. While West Virginia was starting to move away from the Democratic Party, Pat stood on principle and refused to toe any party line. It is likely this crippled his ability to seek higher office, but that was never Pat's objective. His goal was to advance the principles of truth and liberty. The arrogance and foolishness of the legislature and its lack of principle infuriated him. Elected members routinely brushed off his logical arguments. After two years of frustration, Pat removed himself from politics.

Following a short sabbatical, he invited me to West Virginia to help manage his next campaign in 2014. He won a hard-fought battle, but little did we know that the Republican Party would flip the statehouse firmly into its control for the first time since the Great Depression. As a young, attractive, well-spoken, and intelligent member of the legislature, Pat now held an even greater opportunity to gain favor within his party and work towards higher office.

But Pat's ally is truth, and he once again chose to stand with her; that is, he stood alone—or nearly alone. By standing with truth, he drew a few truth-seekers to his side. As leader of a rag-tag coalition known as the 'Liberty Caucus,' Pat was able to throw more than a few monkey wrenches into the warped designs of government central planners. Despite bitter disappointments along an uphill struggle, Pat and his tireless minority defeated numerous proposals ranging from increased taxation to crony regulations—all the while advancing a transparent agenda of personal liberty.

By incorporating Stoicism's teachings, Pat moderated his emotions and made himself a force to be reckoned with. While his political philosophy may not often win allies, the manner in which he conducts himself has won him many admirers. This success and the peace he has found in being a pro-liberty legislator has motivated him to write this book.

Pat has expertly synthesized the Stoic philosophy to build a set of lessons to offer the liberty-oriented statesman. Equally important, his instructions provide a template by which citizens can measure their representatives, regardless of their political beliefs. Finally, liberty-seeking individuals like myself will find that the study of Stoicism can help us achieve some balance within an unfree world.

James Aragon, USAF Ret.
Spring, 2017

Preface

My opening introduction to Stoicism came as a young cadet at the US Air Force Academy, though my initial exposure to the subject was limited. After covering the early Greek philosophers, chiefly Plato and Aristotle, my professor briefly mentioned the Stoics. While short-lived, I can nonetheless recall a very favorable first impression, drawn to the simplicity of the philosophy's neatly-organized compartments, divided between what can and cannot be controlled. During my one and only formal academic class where Stoicism made an appearance, none of the usual suspects showed up. Popular names like Seneca and Marcus Aurelius were omitted for the abbreviated talk, and in the span of maybe half an hour, Stoicism was pitched in generic terms as an old invention of sorts, a unique but perhaps quirky way to approach the world and the problems that come with it.

One name in particular was raised, however, and is more than likely the reason why I remember the discussion from that day at all. Vice Admiral James Stockdale, a highly-decorated US Naval aviator and former prisoner of war, had relied on Stoicism throughout his captivity in North Vietnam. For almost eight years, Admiral Stockdale—the Navy's senior-ranking officer held at the infamous 'Hanoi Hilton'—courageously withstood brutal physical and mental torture, including four years in solitary confinement, two of which were spent in leg irons.

As it happened, I had met James Stockdale the previous year. Then a freshman at the Air Force Academy, I was the 'lowliest of lows.' Just twenty years old, I barely needed to shave in the morning, but I could recognize a rare opportunity. In my mind, Stockdale was larger than life.

Several months before that hasty lesson on Stoicism, the retired admiral at the center of it was visiting campus to deliver a speech on character. Prior to his address, the Medal of Honor winner was making small talk outside the lecture hall, surrounded by a coterie of junior officers and a gaggle of upperclassmen. I had sought out the details ahead of time, taking note of when and where the event was to begin. I distinctly remember not wanting to be late.

I was raised in a household that valued duty. My father, a professional military officer himself, told me stories about Jim Stockdale and other heroic figures before I was old enough to read about them. On a number of occasions, my mother volunteered to host dignitaries and military celebrities at our home, which frequently changed locations in the course of my father's career. Firsthand accounts of aerial dogfights and famous battles were rehashed in our living room by the soldiers and airmen who lived them, including some who had served with Stockdale. When I left for college, I was already well-acquainted with the modern-day Stoic fighter pilot, who had defied the hell of his Vietnamese prison cell.

By the time of my chance encounter with him, Admiral

Stockdale was in the last few years of his life. His steps were slow and awkward, and movement in general looked to be a strenuous task. He leaned on a cane to walk, dragging a crippled knee that had gone untreated by his captors after the high-speed ejection from his downed aircraft. Nearing the age of eighty, the former POW's body was wrecked.

As the only American directly involved in all three of the notorious events in the Gulf of Tonkin, I later read that after his release, Stockdale had spoken out about the misleading incidents used as propaganda to bolster the war in Southeast Asia. The government had lied. The most outrageous deception came from the second episode in the waters of the Tonkin Gulf, which unfolded on the night of August 4th, 1964.

The official US narrative was that North Vietnamese warships had launched an unprovoked attack against a pair of US Naval destroyers. In truth, no shots were fired at the American frigates; the North Vietnamese torpedo boats accused of doing so did not even exist. Flying overhead that night with a bird's-eye view, Stockdale attested to the sham: 'I had the best seat in the house to watch that event, and our destroyers were just shooting at phantom targets…there was nothing there but black water and American fire power.' In the end, Stockdale considered himself a warrior. His role was not to make policy, but to faithfully carry out lawful orders—or as his Stoic coach Epictetus put it two thousand years ago, 'play well the given part.'

Arriving with a few minutes to spare, I managed to push my way through the crowded hall towards the middle of the circle that had formed around the distinguished guest who had yet to enter the auditorium. Stockdale's physical condition may have been failing, but I detected a certain strength in his demeanor, a resolute look in his eyes beneath the human frailty. This was easy to sense because in spite of the momentary glimpse, he looked right at me.

James Stockdale had gained a bit of national fame. Nearly a decade before, he became Ross Perot's running mate in the presidential election of 1992—likely accepting the offer out of a sense of loyalty to a fellow comrade-in-arms—as the independent candidate from Texas also hailed from the US Naval Academy, the admiral's alma mater in Annapolis. Criticism of Perot's losing campaign was especially hard on Stockdale, marked by what was branded as a poor performance in the lone vice-presidential debate of the election season.

At his core, Jim Stockdale was a philosopher. After the Naval Academy, his education on paper consisted of a graduate degree from Stanford where the study of scholars from the past led him to embrace Stoicism. In this context, his sincere public testimony was a reflection of long-standing intellectual insight. It did not make for good television, though, and in the age of thirty second sound bites, it failed to translate on camera. In contrast to the rehearsed answers of smooth politicians sharing the stage, Stockdale's genuine deep-thinking was mocked as confusion from the muddled mind of an old war vet. The sorry result of this fabrication from the media is that many Americans, familiar with James Stockdale, do not remember a man devoted to a lifetime of virtue, but a short skit on *Saturday Night Live*. This was no matter for the Stoic, however; an honest request from a friend had been fulfilled, and what was said afterwards, even on a nationwide scale, was ultimately 'indifferent.'

At the front of the congested gathering now, only a few feet separated me from the fabled resistance leader, who was minutes away from assuming another stage, not to debate the country's politics, but to impart wisdom on a group of college kids just north of Colorado Springs. I was intent on a good seat for his lecture, and anything more was ice cream on my apple pie. Yet in a couple of heartbeats, the thought came to me for an autograph. The only thing with me was my copy of *Contrails*, a small handbook full of famous military quotes and trivia that every cadet in their first year was forced to carry with them (and when pressed, regurgitate its contents from memory). I grabbed it from my back pocket and made eye contact with the man of the hour.

During my quick classroom lesson later the next year, the professor reviewed Jim Stockdale's description of Stoicism, which underscored a mental exercise. Two separate filing cabinets should be formed in the mind, placing everything that can be controlled in the first, and everything that cannot be in the second. Once completed, only things stored in the filing cabinet labeled 'under your control' should receive consideration, while the other should be kept under careful lock and key. The concept was championed by Epictetus, the renowned second-century Stoic instructor whose teachings Stockdale had used to model his own life—a fact I only learned long after my time in college.

On his internment in Vietnam, Stockdale took the ancient Stoic's guidance to heart, recounting his will to focus solely upon the 'filing cabinet' in his power:

> Each individual brings about his own good and
> his own evil, his good fortune, his ill fortune, his
> happiness, and his wretchedness...there can be
> no such thing as being the 'victim' of another.

> You can only be the 'victim' of yourself. It's all
> how you discipline your mind.

The only thing truly under a person's control is the mind. Even in the most extreme circumstances—torture, intimidation, and isolation, with everything else stripped away—Epictetus taught that the individual still retains complete control over the mind and all of the choices that are made from it. This is the understanding of Stoic acumen that Stockdale perfected during his incarceration.

With my cadet manual ready, I ventured away from the edge of the crowd, steering myself toward the opening where the naval commander was headed, steadily limping to the doors of the amphitheater. As I made my way forward, an Air Force captain serving as the admiral's escort for the evening, quickly stepped in front of me, driving out his arm to intercept my approach. Frozen in the center of the donut-shaped gathering, my path now blocked by an overzealous body guard, I made a small gesture for the 'John Hancock' by slightly raising the book in my hand.

For a moment, I thought I had made a serious faux pas. The three-star admiral was one of American history's most decorated members of the armed forces, and with just minutes before his presentation, no one else had dared to intrude his personal space—least of all, some measly little freshman. Maybe I was the one being too eager, and not his aide. In what seemed a longer time than it was, James Stockdale glanced down at the book and then back up at me. Breaking the pause, he waived off his attack dog and motioned for me to come closer. I don't remember saying anything, and I don't know if he did either. In fact, I have no further memories from that night, not even a recollection of his lecture, which he delivered shortly after he was rid of me. I can only recall being present, pleased with the handwriting on the inside flap of my hardback: 'Jim Stockdale, USNA '47.'

The day I came to know Stoicism—and the night I met the man who practiced it—left an impression on my own life in more ways than I could realize at the time. Though I did not adopt the Stoic philosophy until much later, these two experiences in my youth stuck in my mind and helped bring me back to it. By the time I was thirty, I had seen much success, but just as much failure. I was ripe for a 'philosophy of life.'

Elected to the legislature of my native home, logic led to the political philosophy of liberty. Because of the power wielded by the modern-day State, hostility often awaits those in the statehouse with limited-government views. To remain steadfast on values such as private property and free enterprise—and to become more effective at advancing them—a means was needed to deal with this adversity. The same mental faculties of logical reason that dictated my political philosophy also carried me back to Stoicism, not only to confront hardship in my public life, but to improve my personal one as well.

This book is styled in this personal history, but it is not aimed at the warrior like Admiral Stockdale who finds himself stranded behind enemy lines. This work is done for the peacemaker who has come to realize that the source of systematic chaos, poverty, and violence is the State itself—and that the most assured way to 'make peace' is to reverse the growth of government. It is particularly written for those who have not merely diagnosed this social cancer, but are also willing to do something about it.

The heart of this book is advice designed for those who hold office. It is custom-made for public service in any elected assembly, but tailored to those persons boldly committed to free markets and non-intervention—and because of these convictions, are typically labeled constitutionalists, libertarians, or constitutional conservatives. This counsel is offered in the Stoic tradition of Epictetus, derived from his laconic testimonials as conveyed by his student Arrian in the *Enchiridion*. Although the suggestions target a specific audience, anyone facing adversity can apply these concepts within themselves to gain a fuller life and 'persist and resist.'

The first segment gives an overview of the philosophy of Stoicism with a brief history and summary of its major features. It is by no means meant to be an exhaustive or definitive account; the points that are emphasized come from my personal perspective. In this regard, I have used the primary works of Epictetus, Marcus Aurelius, and Seneca—as well as the pieces that are left from the lectures of Musonius Rufus, Epictetus's first-rate teacher in Rome (various translations of these sources were employed, and direct quotations are from aesthetic preference). When appropriate, I have referenced the works of classical scholars to supplement the original sources. The work of A.A. Long is one notable secondary source contributing to my interpretation.

As a case study, I have also included a review of Cato the Younger, the model statesman from antiquity who adhered to Stoicism. Cato's example can reveal a great deal about the Stoic creed in practice, and many lessons of the lived philosophy are reinforced through a closer look at his struggles. Striking parallels between the politics of Cato's day and our own can also be uncovered, which is a valuable element by itself.

Cato's lifetime during the first century BC was the most recorded era of Roman history. Unlike Cicero and Julius Caesar, however, Cato left behind almost nothing from his own hand; a fragment from a letter written to Cicero is all that remains. Cato wrote little to begin with, though, partly owed to the indifference he seemingly held toward his own legacy, an attitude that was not shared by his more well-known contemporaries. Still, it can prove an obstacle in the way of history.

Plutarch's biography is indispensable for such an account, which, if not wholly accurate, provides the most dedicated treatment of Cato's life by a classical historian to survive the ages. I have also drawn from many of Cicero's letters and political speeches, along with Caesar's own take on the civil war that pitted him against the Stoic republican. After this, Cassius Dio's *Roman History*, and Appian's *The Civil Wars* were consulted, as well as the work of other ancient historians.

In addition to the classics, modern secondary sources also aided my interpretation of events. In particular, Anthony Everitt's *Cicero* and Adrian Goldsworthy's *Caesar* were both instrumental to my research. Likewise, *Rome's Last Citizen* by Rob Goodman and Jimmy Soni was an excellent resource, and provided valuable insight into parts of Cato's life. A full reference list of the classical and modern sources appears at the end of this work. I have also included a suggested readings list for those who would like to further their understanding of Stoicism, as well as a guide to some of my favorite works in political philosophy and free-market economics. For ease of reading, footnotes and citations have been omitted throughout the text.

In the *Enchiridion*, Epictetus used a metaphor to explain how all men and women can pursue virtue, regardless of the station they find for themselves in life:

> Remember that you are an actor in a play, and the Playwright chooses the manner of it: If he wants it short, it is short; if long, it is long. If he wants you to act a poor man, you must act the part with all your powers; and so if your part be a cripple or a magistrate or a plain man. For your business is to act the character that is given you and act it well—the choice of the cast is Another's.

Success for a new political ideal can be boosted and enhanced by an old method of personal conduct, and the keys to unlock this end are within reach. If your role in the play is a lover of liberty, the pages of this book can teach you to 'act it well.'

Introduction

Our era is defined by government. Both literally and figuratively, the power of the State has emerged as the supreme force in the modern world. Virtually no category of life is beyond its reach, with the most rudimentary choices no longer left to the individual. How much money you keep, what type of business you can own, and how you live your private life—many of these basic decisions, once simply made by you or your family—are now ultimately determined by government.

Burdensome taxation and the heavy hand of the Nanny State are not the worst of this reality. Throughout the twentieth century, tens of millions of people have been slaughtered in the carnage of the State's wars. Millions were massacred for reasons justified by treacherous pretenses, while millions more perished under internment. These atrocities have not been limited to dictatorships. On the contrary, the world's democracies have been the principal offenders of natural law.

With their invention of total war, twice have the 'civilized' governments annihilated huge swaths of their own population. With mass conscription to carry it out, the indiscriminate targeting of innocent civilians, including women and children, has wiped out entire generations. In the numerous conflicts since these world wars, the death toll and utter devastation to property have reached levels difficult to comprehend. Lord Acton once famously stated, 'Power tends to corrupt,' but to add a caveat to his timeless observation, power also tends to murder and destroy.

Now well into the twenty-first century, history has realized no greater concentration of power than the size and scope of today's institutionalized governments. The steady refinement of fundamental Western precepts—marking the previous millennium—has been turned upside down. The political trend culminating in the modern nation-state is a result of this implosion, a collapse of sound ideals marching civilization backwards. Undoing this accumulation of power is vital to the peace and prosperity of the future.

Social change, though, ultimately rests upon a point that should not be underappreciated: ideas matter. For a large portion of Americans, very dangerous propositions have once again been embraced, and in spite of their many labels to the opposite, these degenerate ideas are anything but new and progressive. In one fashion or another, these are the antiquated concepts of omnipotent authority.

Ideas which advance government power are essential to this 'decivilizing' regression, for its continued growth requires public acceptance. The rise of the Almighty State is only enabled through ideas, approved or disapproved in the minds of men and women. Though they may be called different names, above all else, these firmly-entrenched notions promote centralized authority.

Once the venue of powerful government is established, expanding its magnitude can be done with ever-increasing ease.

For this tendency to continue unchecked, though, Plato's 'noble lie' must always be advanced, for the enlargement of the State hinges on the public's willingness to abdicate more of their sovereignty.

Because the enormity of the State, along with the actions it pursues, is widely considered 'legitimate,' there are few hard limits to its power. Far superior to written constitutions, ideas serve as the only real checks to government. Perverted ideals endowed it with supremacy in the first place, but with the right ideas, the State loses its claim on legitimacy—and with this loss, its activity, growth, and very existence as a dominating force becomes threatened.

Since ideas are paramount, rolling back state power hinges first on the right ones. Championing this cause, a tiny minority has emerged, dedicated to the philosophy of individual political liberty. Though the American tradition started around this premise, in the context of human history, it constitutes a very new development.

This 'liberty movement' consists of a collection of individuals from different walks of life, committed towards a mutual principle. Coalesced around a common objective, these liberty lovers have grasped the only philosophy both morally and practically capable of confronting the heart of the political struggle in the modern age. To be effective in such an ordeal pitted against the State, a method of personal conduct should be adopted for those undertaking the task—one that is best suited for the arduous road ahead.

First, what exactly does it mean to be a liberty lover? For many, it begins with an awakening of sorts. A dawning on the human consciousness comes to light, beginning with the realization that among all of society's organizations, the State is uniquely peculiar.

As the lone institution that can systematically rob and murder without consequence, the State is the primary culprit behind poverty and pervasive unrest within modern society, causing many of the gross depravities commonly seen today.

Individual liberty drives toward the opposite of these horrid ends, categorically bringing about higher standards of morality and superior utility. Free men and women, cooperating peacefully through the division of labor and the voluntary exchange of their own property—without the initiation of force—produce not only the greatest degree of social prosperity, but an ethical framework with the strongest claims on justice. To love liberty is to love civilization.

Many of today's attacks on liberty lovers come from a place of arrogance; political liberty is an ideology for misguided kids, not for adults. While one is 'young and dumb,' the writings of Frédéric Bastiat or Murray Rothbard can be captivating. But, say the critics, everyone must eventually mature and abandon such foolish thoughts.

The reverse of this ritual disparagement is true. The path to social peace and human flourishing is found within individual liberty. The State tends to restrict the freedom of thought, ownership, and action—depriving the world of innovation, wealth, and progress. Naivety rests with those who would desert these certainties, and who so often succumb to what F.A. Hayek coined 'the fatal conceit.'

In this political struggle, the adversary of liberty is not so much other men and women. Neither is it necessarily the individuals who staff the bureaucracies of the government itself. The true foe is not the despot, but his propaganda: the backwards and even sinister designs that demand a solution to society's problems by the central authority. These ideas are the enemy, and not simply to those within the liberty movement. They are the enemy of civilization.

This movement towards liberty has been steadily growing, though unfortunately not as fast as government. Nevertheless, optimism has a strong case. In large thanks to Congressman Ron Paul, many have a better grasp of liberty, as well as a deeper understanding of the immorality and irrational destruction of the State. Interest in free-market economics and the political thought of 'classical liberalism' is at an all-time high.

Today, more people are studying Ludwig von Mises and his fellow 'Austrians' than ever before. The consequences of 'blowback' from the District of Columbia's foreign wars are now a conventional consideration, and the Federal Reserve, once a sacred cow off limits to mainstream debate, is correctly becoming more recognized as the State's legal counterfeiting tool. For a new generation of Americans, this great intellectual heritage of the near past has been rediscovered. In a sense, a small modern-day renaissance has been unleashed, and as dismal as the future may sometimes appear, this is progress worthy of celebration.

However, this development also raises a pivotal question. With record numbers educated in the literature of liberty, how is this newfound knowledge to be applied? Thomas Jefferson's torch may be reignited, but now the flame must be carried ahead. After all, it's one thing to learn about these ideas. It's quite another to put them into practice. Oftentimes, individuals become enamored with their 'enlightenment,' but are quickly disenfranchised from supporting a losing political campaign or after their phone calls are dismissed by their district representatives. Initial motivation can easily dissipate once resistance is met.

Others take no tangible action beyond resigning themselves to typing away on social media. Although well-meant, this over-passionate mold of political engagement is not only unproductive, but counterproductive, as these 'Facebook warriors' often rudely respond in public settings to those who disagree, potentially alienating would-be allies. Conversely, some who do take larger steps forward, run for office to advance these convictions, but once elected, they are habitually corrupted by the temptations of power, lured into forsaking the very principles they set out to defend. In short, the forces arrayed against these ideas are very steep. Even the most dedicated friends of liberty can be overwhelmed, enraged, or compromised by the immense adversity liberty ultimately faces.

Notwithstanding, liberty lovers have assumed leading roles in combating state power, building the bridge between the theory of the philosophy and its implementation. To further the undertaking, many have participated in successful political campaigns or have achieved office themselves. Whether these individuals be the office holders or their personal advisers, what to do next can be vexing, and sometimes, deeply unnerving. But it need not be. As Marcus Aurelius put it, 'Never let the future disturb you. You will meet it, if you have to, with the same weapons of reason which today arm you against the present.' There is no better means of conduct in which to fight the primeval idea of omnipotent government than through the old tried-and-tested philosophy of Stoicism.

As the political philosophy of liberty is grounded in reason and logic, so too is Stoicism. If you purport that the highest levels of rationality would leave society to spontaneously order itself, then you must align your own behavior with this same mental tenet. Cicero may have concurred when he wrote, 'He who is to live in accordance with nature must base his principles upon the system and government of the entire world.'

Stressing virtue, Stoicism endorses consistency and not compromise. It is a moral way of life first, but also serves with utility by its revelation that the individual is inherently possessed with all the tools necessary to achieve happiness and inner serenity. Its practice also prevents negative emotions such as anger and fear from interfering with sound judgment, a handy feature under the statehouse when duty calls.

Another valuable component of Stoicism in public office is the philosophy's adherence to principle. Many Stoics from history are famous for their principled stands, most notably Cato the Younger (as you can later discover in this book). This beneficial element thwarts the corruption of personal integrity, which is perhaps the most critical to the advancement of political liberty. What's more, Stoic thought developed the very groundwork upon which the philosophy of liberty rests, such as natural law and the proportionality ethic of justice. It is all the more suitable to personally adopt the philosophy which gave birth to the doctrine of political liberty.

Stoicism is demanding, but so is devotion to political liberty. The advice in this book is not popular, but just as the principles of liberty can often be out of favor, you must learn to shun populism and cling only to 'right reason.' In this fashion, you will find the counsel offered to be fully opposed to Saul Alinsky's manual, *Rules for Radicals*—both in form, by renouncing the dishonorable tactics and vices the fanatic sanctioned, as well as the rejection of the crazed, animalistic ideology he sought to accelerate.

The statehouse is a very personal atmosphere, and every day, you will face irrational men and women in close quarters who vehemently condemn your positions—and oftentimes you as a person. Because of the crowded physical proximity of such a setting, and the collective group-think mentality built into elected assemblies, the defense of liberty-minded First Principles will frequently lead to vicious confrontations. To stay the course, you must overcome your lurking predisposition to cede ground simply to avoid uncomfortable social interactions. It is only natural to want to be liked, but you must value your convictions more than your baser desires to get along. Admiral Jim Stockdale summed this up well:

> If you want to protect yourself from 'fear and guilt,' and those are the crucial pincers, the real long-term destroyers of will, you have to get rid of all your instincts to compromise, to meet people halfway. You have to learn to stand aloof, never give openings for deals, never level with your adversaries.

Stoicism can help you become a steadfast example. It does not require 'populism' to make an impact—only the truth. In fact, one individual with enough commitment can sway an entire multitude of their peers. In the long run, such exemplary dedication can influence a nation. As Lord Acton pronounced, 'At all times, sincere friends of freedom have been rare and its triumphs have been due to minorities...' Master the Stoic art, and you can be this resolute minority.

PART I

Stoicism

A Way of Life

"We, not externals, are the masters of our judgments."
— *Epictetus*

Stoicism

Background and the objective of virtue

Stoicism is an ancient philosophy, first appearing in Athens around the year 300 BC. Founded by Zeno of Citium, it became a leading school of thought in the Greco-Roman world. Zeno and his followers attracted large audiences at the *Stoa*, a covered porch decorated with murals of mythical battles on the northern edge of the Athenian marketplace. For hundreds of years, young Greeks and Romans could attend these public lectures, which offered a systematic method of living—and in particular, a means to confront hardship.

Like most of the Greek splinter schools of the Hellenistic period, Stoicism has its roots in Socratic philosophy. In the age preceding the birth of Stoicism, Socrates posited that virtue— or excellent living—was worth doing in its own right. While Plato and Aristotle would cover broad areas of knowledge in the century after his life, the Stoics would hone their attention on this initial Socratic point.

Virtue for the Stoics consisted not merely in doing what was morally right, with the right intentions, but in exercising virtue in all manners of living. Unlike the modern-day philosophy of academia, consumed by minutiae and inherently disinterested with practical application, the Stoics concerned themselves with actually living. Emphasizing practice over pure theory, virtue became this life objective, with the acquisition of knowledge always supporting this goal. In what would become doctrine, Zeno's immediate successors, Cleanthes and later Chrysippus, the authority of early Stoicism, neatly summarized the good life's formula: 'Live in accordance with nature.'

The recipe within this phrase contains the logic of virtue. 'Nature' for the Stoics was not used in the same context as its modern meaning, but carried a different connotation. Rather than the origin of a thing, the Stoics connected nature with a thing's end. In other words, nature did not signify the natural state of something, but its highest capacity for perfection or flourishment. If man was to live according to his nature, he must do so rationally, for man's paramount natural characteristic is his ability to reason, the premier feature distinguishing him from beasts.

But why the pursuit of virtue? Proceeding from the Socratic axiom that virtue has value in itself, its attainment should be motivated without the prospect of reward or from fear of punishment, but for its own sake. As man's unique trait of reason is the highest ability of his own nature, reason reveals that to properly fulfill this potential, he must do so with excellent character and effort. For man to be consistent with nature, he must adopt the ways of virtue.

Moral excellence, happiness, and duty

With this groundwork came a more utilitarian purpose: to be happy, one must be virtuous. Stoicism developed Socratic virtue, as not only an end in itself, but the only end which mattered. Breaking with Aristotle, the Stoics postulated that happiness rested on virtuous living alone. Just as the accurate meaning of 'nature' can be lost in translation, so too can their picture of happiness. In the Stoic sense, happiness is not limited to a narrow feeling of delight, but conveys a wider state of internal well-being—the overall health of the soul. Doing what is right, with correct reason, provides clearness of conscience. When virtuous intention and action are consistently chosen, an individual can be secure with the comforting self-awareness of obtaining the only genuine good, intrinsically valuable in its own right. No matter how much fame or how many riches are gained, without virtue, corruption of the soul festers—troubling man from the inside. The absence of virtue then also leads to a deficiency of true happiness.

On the other hand, wealth and reputation are fleeting; a man's honor can only be lost from his own accord. By adhering to virtue, the well-being of the soul can persevere through impoverishment, hatred from others, physical pain, or bodily disease. As St. Thomas Aquinas put it in the thirteenth century, 'Happiness is secured through virtue; it is a good attained by man's own will.'

The Stoics divided virtue into categories, building the later Christian framework for the four cardinal virtues: wisdom, self-control, courage, and justice. The latter grouping reflects Stoic reasoning that man is a social animal, with certain responsibilities innate to the good life. Concerning the associations with our fellow man, exercising justice requires honest transactions, especially the integrity of the spoken word, as well as benevolence toward others, and the sincere maintenance of fraternal relations. Because man's nature includes obligations—first to family and friends, and then, when fully extended, to mankind in general— duty is at the center of virtue.

Of course, cultivating virtue under the bonds of social commitment can bring conflict and distress. Because of this inevitability, the ways of the *Stoa* rest on the maxim famously forwarded by Epictetus, the gifted philosopher from the days of the Roman Empire. Stoics like Epictetus counseled the observance of an overarching principle, to discount what cannot be controlled, giving care solely to the things that can be.

In the end, only the individual can deviate from the moral path of excellence, for the pursuit of virtue is not subject to anything outside of the individual's power. The good life then falls entirely to the individual, with no excuses, even in the most extreme circumstances and conditions. Since the lone ingredient to true happiness is virtue, this too remains independent of 'externals.' To live according to nature, an individual's focus must first be inward, to guard and improve his own inner state of well-being.

What precisely is within this power? What is 'up to us'? Friends, family, property, material possessions, and a person's own body can be influenced by external forces and, therefore, lie outside individual control. The mind alone, and what directly results from it, is the exclusive sovereign. These mental derivatives include an individual's thoughts, opinions, judgments, desires, choices, and actions—or in a word, a person's will. If attention is carefully kept within this spectrum, men and women can shield themselves from the 'slings and arrows of outrageous fortune.' Stretched beyond it, such a defenseless individual can become debilitated or distraught, and not simply distracted from the goal of virtue, but left with an inability to determine what the virtuous goal should be.

What is more, squandering time and energy fretting over that which a person is powerless can severely depreciate the virtue of self-control, turning unproductive disturbances into counterproductive devastation. Avoiding attachments to those things tied to the influence of outside forces not only preserves sound judgment, but wards off negative emotions and the destructive behavior that comes with them. Immaterial to the good life, these externals to our mental faculty must be grasped as indifferent, otherwise the individual can also cave to the passions.

Equanimity of mind

Of particular concern for the Stoics are negative emotions: anger, fear, hatred, jealousy, and lust. These represent the basest human feelings—potentially destructive vices in themselves and crippling obstacles in the way of virtuous progress. Practicing the virtue of self-control prevents the generation of these irrational passions, and the Stoics devised a meticulous strategy to accomplish this end.

Beginning with the standard of strict focus upon only the

things within personal control, observations made throughout the course of the day are to be properly evaluated, giving assent to these impressions only after they are judged to be true. To put it without Stoic terminology, things are often not what they seem, so it makes little sense to impulsively jump to conclusions.

For instance, suppose an event in life does not turn out as expected or a friend acts in an otherwise unfriendly manner. Instead of accepting the initial impression, 'this happened and it is annoying,' weigh the matter for what it really is by dropping the immediate conclusion 'and it is annoying.' By mentally dissecting external events and actions from others, a domain in which one has no control, what is left is one plain fact: 'this happened.'

All disturbances or distractions leading to vice were held by the Stoics to be poor value-judgments of a person's observations. To be consistent with reason, man's highest nature, impressions from the senses must be correctly interpreted (and in this light, the Stoics are very much Aristotelians, asserting that reality can be determined through experience). Once false impressions are rejected and assent only given to truth, the individual can proceed with certainty, to act in line with virtue, toward the virtuous goal.

Cognitive discipline requires practice to master, but it became a trick of the Stoic trade. The leading thinkers of the philosophy were all-too-aware of the distress frequently caused by false value-judgments attached to trivial affairs—as the psychological insight from Epictetus notably pointed out, 'Man is affected, not by events, but by the view he takes of them.' After it is realized that the mind can be sharpened to see things for what they are, the quality of thoughts can improve. Likewise, the use of this high-caliber reasoning, to achieve clear and calm thinking, can help drive away the irrational passions before they mentally form.

At the core of the ruling faculty's training is the regulation of desire and aversion, including the distinction between the 'good' and the 'bad.' What is truly good should be sought, and only what is truly bad shunned. A true good is always under the individual's control and 'in accordance with nature,' while a true bad is within the individual's control, but unnatural or opposed to reason.

When these values of the good and bad are kept intact, both desire and aversion can be satisfied, since the individual simply fulfills the one while rejecting the other. If, however, values are misplaced, then individuals will find themselves chasing the unattainable or evading the inescapable. This pointless exercise invariably results in disappointment, and can shatter a person's quest for virtue and the good life.

Perhaps the most common causes of this destructive futility involve pain and pleasure—externals that should be regarded as indifferent to the virtuous life—but are generally confused as good or bad themselves. When pleasure and pain become the desired good and the avoided bad, irrational attachments are established that eventually create misery, as both are subject to the shifting winds of fortune, unresponsive to the individual's commands. Indulging in too much pleasure also degrades the virtue of self-control, just as an irrational fear of pain can paralyze many from their commitments.

Moreover, for a Stoic, at times it may be necessary to endure severe suffering, without any comfort, in order to achieve the virtuous end. Correct and consistent values stave off attachments to indifferent goods, which can otherwise preclude the individual from his or her duty.

With this approach, the practice of Stoicism also yields peace of mind, a byproduct of rational thought. By making progress toward virtue, an inner calmness becomes the standard mental state, especially as the quality of Stoic skill improves. Honing the abilities to judge the truth of impressions, maintain the proper ends of desire and aversion, and above all, confine care to what can be controlled, disturbance is replaced with tranquility—further aiding clarity of purpose.

The origins of Western thought

Although Epictetus and other leading figures of Stoicism are known for promoting a way of life, their comprehensive worldview also advanced vital Western principles. Plato and Aristotle had established political theories stuck in the collectivist quagmire of the *polis*, or Greek city-state. Unable to move past their statist environment, little distinction was made between State and society. Molded together, the lack of separation generally equated the two, whereas the State became society. Diverging from these models, Stoicism's treatment of the individual enabled a new way of thought, helping to throw off the mental shackles of the State.

Through the logical analysis that all individuals were interconnected by their natural possession of reason, linking each member of mankind with Providence, it followed that certain universal principles preempted any government laws or man-made decrees. Leveling the 'Kantian imperative' nearly two millennia before Immanuel Kant, a natural law was applied to all individuals, not just to some—and encompassed all states, not simply a select few. Stoic thought conceived these ethical prerogatives without limit to time and place. As constants, their validity remained immune to the incidental variables of when and where.

Foremost among these standards was that government had a moral obligation to protect life and property, which prohibited murder and theft by extension. Therefore, actions that were unjust for private citizens were also unjust for government officials. Regardless of title or rank, no one was above this natural law.

From this tradition, the philosophy inspired some of the most noteworthy intellectuals from antiquity, including a number of figures who shaped the course of history. Names like Cicero and Cato come to mind. Serving as Emperor Nero's chief adviser, Seneca produced the bulk of the surviving work about Stoic ethics, and his letters are still considered to be some of the best prose ever assembled from this era. And according to some sources, Epictetus was more famous in his day than Plato was in his. In fact, so celebrated was Epictetus that the Emperor Hadrian himself personally paid a visit to the slave-turned-philosopher.

With the accession of Marcus Aurelius to the throne, a 'philosopher-king' stood at the head of the Roman Empire. The last of Niccolò Machiavelli's 'five good emperors,' the eighteenth-century historian Edward Gibbon had this to say about the Stoic ruler in his classic study, *The History of the Decline and Fall of the Roman Empire*:

> At the age of twelve years, he embraced the rigid
> system of the Stoics, which taught him to submit
> his body to his mind, his passions to his reason;

to consider virtue as the only good, vice as the
only evil, all things external as things indifferent.

Indeed, it is with Marcus where the most widely-read Stoic
literature originated—his journal, the *Meditations*. By his reign
late in the second century, Stoicism had reached the pinnacle of
its influence.

Though formal instruction in the philosophy came to an
end in the early sixth century, Stoicism left a legacy that lives
on to this day. For instance, several aspects of Christianity have
deep-seated Stoic themes, as many of the early Church Fathers
were heavily predisposed to Stoic thought. And in the field of
modern psychology, cognitive-behavioral therapy, a commonly
used treatment for mental disorders, was inspired by none other
than Stoicism.

In spite of this impact, purposefully using the philosophy as
a way of life is scarcely detectible today. Outside the few snippets
a college student may come by in the classroom, most people
have no exposure to the subject—and if they do, such knowledge
is typically restricted to the mistaken view that to be Stoic is to
repress emotion.

Nevertheless, for hundreds of years in the West, these Stoic
giants from the past were still studied—or at the very least,
publicly familiar to society at large. In fact, up until the late
1800's, Cicero's book *On Duties* was mandatory reading for
many high school students in the United States. By the turn of
the twentieth century, though, the rise of public schools brought
about the downfall of classical education. As a result, these
monumental individuals who left such a great mark on history
have been largely forgotten.

Stoicism's influence runs deeper than what many historians will credit. Besides establishing a way of life for personal conduct within society, the philosophy left an enormous impression on how society itself should be organized. With Stoic logic framing natural law, a pervasive social contribution was made, which laid the foundation of liberty for the modern world. To this end, Stoic reasoning emphatically swayed a broad number of the West's greatest scholars. St. Thomas Aquinas, Hugo Grotius, René Descartes, Adam Smith, and the Baron de Montesquieu were all energized by Stoicism's rationale, guiding Western political thought from the Middle Ages to the Enlightenment. In truth, the core of man's intellectual progress was shaped by Stoicism.

But these innovations in thought were hammered out by the men who first carried them. Learning more about these early Stoic individuals is valuable, not only because the fundamentals of liberty were constructed by the principles they adopted, but because they are commendable role models in their own right. What is more, meaningful abstract ideas are sometimes best understood by the study of those who embodied them. One such individual worth studying, especially under the context of the statehouse, was a Roman who both lived and died 'according to nature': Cato the Younger.

Chronology

Some years approximate

399 BC   Death of Socrates

380 BC   Plato writes his *Republic*

350 BC   Aristotle invents logic with his *Prior Analytics*

348 BC   Death of Plato

343 BC   Aristotle begins to tutor Alexander the Great

340 BC   Aristotle's *Nicomachean Ethics* composed

323 BC   Death of Alexander the Great

322 BC   Death of Aristotle

300 BC   Zeno of Citium begins lecturing the new philosophy of Stoicism in Athens

262 BC   Cleanthes becomes head of the Stoic school in Athens, following Zeno's death

234 BC   Birth of Cato the Elder near Rome

230 BC   Chrysippus succeeds Cleanthes as the third head of the Stoic school in Athens

218 BC	Hannibal crosses the Alps and invades Roman Italy
202 BC	Scipio Africanus defeats Hannibal in North Africa
195 BC	Cato the Elder serves as elected consul
149 BC	Death of Cato the Elder
146 BC	Rome destroys the city of Carthage
146 BC	Roman conquests of Greece and Macedonia
133 BC	Tiberius Gracchus killed in Rome following his populist land redistribution laws
115 BC	Birth of Marcus Crassus
107 BC	Marius transforms Roman army into a professional standing force
106 BC	Birth of Cicero
106 BC	Birth of Pompey the Great
100 BC	Birth of Julius Caesar
95 BC	Birth of Cato the Younger
88 BC	King Mithridates orchestrates the 'Asiatic Vespers,' massacring thousands of Roman civilians in Asia Minor
88 BC	Sulla marches legions into Rome
86 BC	Death of Marius
82 BC	Sulla's dictatorship begins; his proscriptions carried out
81 BC	Sulla relinquishes power
78 BC	Death of Sulla
73 BC	Slave uprising by Spartacus and fellow gladiators

72 BC	Publicola given command of an army; Cato serves as staff officer
71 BC	Spartacus defeated by Marcus Crassus
70 BC	Pompey the Great and Crassus serve as co-consuls
68 BC	Mutiny by Lucullus's legions in the East
67 BC	Cato serves as an elected military tribune; commands a legion in Macedonia
66 BC	Senate replaces Lucullus with Pompey as commander of armies in the East
65 BC	Cato leaves the army and returns to Rome; elected quaestor
64 BC	Cato prosecutes participants from Sulla's proscriptions
63 BC	Cicero's consulship; Catiline conspiracy put down in Rome
63 BC	Death of King Mithridates
62 BC	Catiline's army crushed; Catiline killed in battle
61 BC	Pompey returns to Rome after defeating King Mithridates and settling the East
60 BC	First Triumvirate forms (alliance between Caesar, Pompey, and Crassus)
59 BC	Julius Caesar serves as elected consul, along with Bibulus
59 BC	Grain dole becomes free of charge for Roman populace

58 BC	Caesar begins his proconsul governorship in Gaul; Gallic wars begin
58 BC	Cato leaves to oversee Roman annexation of Cyprus
56 BC	Cato returns to Rome
55 BC	Pompey and Crassus serve their second elected consulship
54 BC	Cato serves as elected praetor
54 BC	Pompey's wife Julia (Caesar's daughter) dies in childbirth
53 BC	Crassus killed invading Parthian Empire
52 BC	Pompey named sole consul in Rome
52 BC	Cato loses his election for the consulship
51 BC	Cicero publishes *On the Republic*
49 BC	Caesar crosses the Rubicon; Roman civil war erupts
48 BC	Pompey defeated by Caesar at the Battle of Pharsalus; Pompey murdered in Egypt
48 BC	Cato leads remaining republican resistance to Utica in North Africa
46 BC	Caesar destroys republican forces under Metellus Scipio at the Battle of Thapsus
46 BC	Suicide of Cato the Younger in Utica
44 BC	Julius Caesar proclaimed dictator for life
44 BC	Caesar assassinated in Rome on the Ides of March
43 BC	Cicero murdered by Marc Antony's men

42 BC	Octavian and Marc Antony overcome Brutus and Cassius at the Battle of Philippi
31 BC	Marc Antony and Cleopatra defeated by Octavian at the Battle of Actium
27 BC	Octavian becomes the Emperor Augustus; establishes Roman monarchy
19 BC	Virgil's *Aeneid* published, praising Cato's piety and principle
4 BC	Birth of Seneca
55 AD	Seneca writes *On the Firmness of the Wise Man* (with Cato as the model sage)
55 AD	Birth of Epictetus
61 AD	Lucan begins drafting the *Pharsalia*, employing Cato as his chronicle's heroic figure
65 AD	Seneca forced to commit suicide by the Emperor Nero
69 AD	Musonius Rufus teaches Stoicism in Rome; Epictetus is among his students
121 AD	Birth of Marcus Aurelius
125 AD	Arrian publishes the *Enchiridion*, from the lectures of Epictetus
135 AD	Death of Epictetus
161 AD	Marcus Aurelius becomes emperor of Roman Empire
180 AD	Marcus Aurelius dies; his *Meditations* later released

PART II

Cato the Younger

Reviewing the Life of a Stoic Statesman

"It will even do to socialize with men of good character, in order to model your life on theirs, whether you choose someone living or someone from the past."
— *Epictetus*

Cato the Younger

Early life and legacy

In the depths of the winter of 1778, within a small hideaway situated in southeastern Pennsylvania, thousands of exhausted colonial soldiers withered away from sickness and starvation. With little shelter from the cold, they faced enormous odds. Even if they survived the disease-ridden camp, the enemy's well-rested forces were gathering in overwhelming numbers inside the warm quarters of nearby Philadelphia, determined to crush the fledgling rebellion once the snow lifted.

In the midst of this despair, the commander of the American continental army decided, of all things, to stage a theatrical play. To boost morale, George Washington ordered the performance of a drama, a chronicle covering the struggles of a Roman senator who lived nearly two thousand years before the bitter ordeal at Valley Forge—a story that may have helped inspire the American rabble to endure their own suffering. Only a short time later, Washington's tired troops emerged from the harsh Pennsylvania winter, eventually securing victory over the British military.

The Roman at the center of this Stoic saga was Cato the

Younger—history's most famous foe of authoritarian power, who to his end opposed one-man rule, including Julius Caesar's new world order. George Washington revered him, as did many of his peers, including John Adams and Benjamin Franklin. In fact, some of the best-known lines from this Revolutionary Era— such as Patrick Henry's, 'Give me liberty or give me death' and Nathan Hale's, 'I only regret that I have but one life to lose for my country'—were actually lifted from Joseph Addison's script, *Cato: A Tragedy in Five Acts*, the very same pop-theater that Washington had used to motivate his men at Valley Forge.

But it was not only the generation of America's founders that held the Stoic senator in such high esteem. Throughout the ages following his death, the tremendous impact of Cato's life is hard to measure. Looking back on his own intellectual heritage, the imperial-Stoic Seneca described Cato as the only man to reach the status of 'sage'—a Greek label for the completely virtuous individual.

Cato would also be romanticized by the greatest poets of the ancient world. Virgil immortalized him in his Roman epic, the *Aeneid*, while later, Seneca's nephew Lucan celebrated the Stoic republican as the hero of his first-century masterpiece, the *Pharsalia*. In fact, Cato's memory during this period served as inspiration to men who formed the backbone of resistance to the Emperor Nero's tyranny.

By the fourteenth century, one of the few pagans Dante honored in his *Divine Comedy* was Cato, who in the classic medieval poem, was charged by the Almighty with guarding the gates of Purgatory. And in the early 1700's, *Cato's Letters* were composed by a pair of Englishmen to protest unjust laws and oppressive government underneath the swollen British Empire.

For several years, well over one hundred of John Trenchard's and Thomas Gordon's essays circulated in print with England's largest newspapers—all of which bore Cato's name. Just who exactly was this Roman from antiquity who left such a legacy?

If Stoicism had a patron saint, it would without a doubt be Marcus Porcius Cato. To distinguish him from his ancestor, he is today commonly known as Cato the Younger. In Rome during the early first century BC, however, Cato may have initially seemed to lack the wits for anything beyond an ordinary life. The early death of his parents left Cato in the care of his uncle, and his famous biographer Plutarch reported that when it came to his education, the young orphan 'was sluggish of comprehension and slow, but what he comprehended he held fast in his memory.'

Cato was the direct descendent of a legendary statesman. His great-grandfather was the Roman equivalent of a self-made man, who managed to enter politics from his meager plebeian standing and eventually achieved the highest office in the Republic— earning the family line the noble title 'Cato,' signifying wisdom and experience. Because of his aristocratic birth, expectations for the younger Cato were high. He did not disappoint.

Cato came to Stoicism as an adolescent. After formal lessons were finished, it was typical of Romans from the upper-class to familiarize themselves with the philosophy taught in Greece, which had become a symbol of status for the Roman elite. By this time, Athens had produced a wide range of competing schools of thought, and expensive Greek tutors were hired by Roman nobility to give their youth a sense of refinement and culture. Philosophy was becoming vogue inside the Roman capital, and patrician households commonly selected instructors trained in the more fashionable schools founded by Epicurus and Plato.

Many of Cato's contemporaries approached the Greek import with a cavalier attitude, buying the luxury good without mentally adopting it. This carefree sentiment can be realized through the type of tutor that was chosen. The self-indulgent philosophy of the Epicureans professed that pleasure and comfort should be the ultimate pursuit in life, while the proto-nihilism of Plato's disciples, the Skeptics, typically led to bickering over vain abstractions with little regard to practical living. Romans of high birth were often eclectic with these varying ideas, hiring multiple tutors, and selectively taking what they found agreeable from each. It was precisely this lifestyle which Cato's great-grandfather had admonished a century before, scorning Greek philosophy as effeminate rubbish that belonged in Athens. Carrying his famous ancestor's views, Cato would shun philosophy for culture. However, he would adopt philosophy for discipline—a course his great-grandfather would have approved of.

By the younger Cato's day, Stoicism was coming to be held in high esteem. Compared to its competitors though, the Stoic school remained an uncommon area of study, and even more infrequently practiced—more than likely because it was also the most demanding. Much like Stoicism itself, Cato was less interested in philosophy as a conversation piece and more emphatic in living it.

Stoicism matched his core inclinations, as seen through the way he chose to live. In spite of his large inheritance, affording him the ease of a carefree lifestyle, Cato opted for a frugal existence. He drank the cheapest wine, kept to a mundane diet, and while others rode on horseback, Cato walked—sometimes barefoot.

He was not only thrifty, but went out of his way to make

himself uncomfortable, sticking to a vigorous exercise regimen. He forwent warm clothing in the cold, and proper shade in the heat. When he was ill, he did not complain, but quietly accepted his condition of ailment. He not only rejected extravagance, he spurned luxury as a distraction from virtue. The fashionable purple tunic, which Romans of the 'best families' wore to show off their wealth, was never seen on Cato. Instead, he wore a simple toga, which harkened back to the days of his conservative ancestors. His unusual habits surely produced gossip, but as Plutarch recounts, Cato remained silent to such criticism, 'accustoming himself to be ashamed only of what was really shameful, and to ignore men's low opinion of other things.'

Cato volunteers for the army

Following his older brother's example, Cato joined the Roman army as a staff officer. The slave uprising led by Spartacus and his gladiators was quickly accelerating into a full-fledged war, and as the slaves dispatched one Roman army after the next, the Senate franticly moved to squash the rebellion. A pair of armies were formed to end the revolt, and Cato's military service began by advising Lucius Gellius Poplicola, a high-ranking Roman politician appointed to command one of these sizeable forces. Though Poplicola proved unsuccessful at bringing the uprising to an end, his legions inflicted more damage to Spartacus's slaves than any other field army to that point (Spartacus was finally defeated by a combined force of several legions, led by Marcus Crassus, the wealthiest man in Roman history, who had the surviving slaves crucified alongside a main road to Rome).

After the campaign concluded, Poplicola, who would later stand behind Cato's political faction in the Senate, offered to decorate the young officer for his bravery in combat. To perhaps test his own resistance to flattery, Plutarch summed up the answer Cato gave to his future political supporter: 'Cato would not take them nor allow them, declaring that he had done nothing worthy of honors.' The Stoic turned down the medals.

By the first century BC, Roman military campaigns were long affairs, sometimes lasting for years. Gone were the days of Rome's fabled citizen-soldier, when farmers in the tradition of Cincinnatus would put down their plows to defend the homeland. Volunteer troops traditionally furnished their own weapons and equipment, and unlike professional legionaries, citizen-soldiers had little incentive for adventurism; time away from the farm was costly. From their common occupational backgrounds, a shared interest emerged, which typically went no further than internal security. Even when forced conscription was used, as it so often was in ancient Rome, once the foreign threat had passed, these men of the middle class wasted no time agitating for a speedy return to their farm work.

By Cato's era, however, neighboring threats to Rome had been extinguished by previous generations—the most notorious being Hannibal's invasion forces, which were not only crushed, but at the behest of Cato's own great-grandfather, the city of Carthage itself had been wiped out in a fit of retribution (regardless of the subject, Cato the Elder would famously conclude every speech he gave in his later years with 'Moreover,

Carthage must be destroyed'). Roman policy had steadily grown into offensive expansion, and one by one, the old familiar powers of the Mediterranean world, left in the wake of Alexander the Great, were conquered by the new Roman force. The extent of this empire was becoming so vast that a professional army was needed to maintain it.

The political dynamics of this transition should not be underappreciated. To fill the ranks of a standing army, the masses of the urban plebs were used. These commoners held no property and had little in the way of particular skill sets. Full-time service in the army came with scanty public pay, but it included fringe benefits. These entailed the spoils of conquest and the promise of land grants after enlistments were completed. Loyalty no longer rested conceptually with a 'return to normalcy,' but more literally, with the arbitrary whims of the commander in the field. Professional soldiers who expected plunder and loot bred a new government interest group. But even more unsettling, thousands of battle-hardened warriors, loyal to one man, created a powerful weapon to achieve personal and political gain—constitution, written or unwritten, be damned. The Republic was already yielding symptoms of systemic fracture, and this was the environment that Cato the Younger stepped into when in the year 67 BC, he accepted his first command over a legion in Macedonia.

By the time he arrived at his last military station, Cato had honed his Stoic practices. With his study of the philosophy, he was also dedicated to its constant exercise—and not just through his unconventional living habits. By declining war medals, he established his disdain for vanity. He had also begun to highlight his adherence to the rule of law, which he would demonstrate throughout the rest of his life.

During an election for military tribune, in which a collection of officers was regularly elected to command troops in the field, Cato was said to be the only candidate to follow the regulation requiring those who stood for public office to campaign without nomenclators. It was the job of these personal escorts, with their reliable memories, to discreetly supply pertinent small-talk material while the candidate attended formal functions or mingled with guests at meet-and-greets. No Roman went without them, and though the statute was not enforced, making certain that these critical social 'cheats' could be used irrespective of the law, Cato obeyed the rule all the same—and won the campaign on the strength of his own merit. As he arrived for duty in Macedonia (present-day Bulgaria and northern Greece), his budding reputation for honesty already preceded him.

Command in the field

Roman military service in Macedonia was no country-club assignment. The region had a storied history of warfare, and in particular, one which had violently opposed Rome's rule. Not only had it been the birthplace of Alexander the Great, but late in the third century BC, the Kingdom of Macedon had allied with Rome's archenemies, the Carthaginians. Hannibal was scarcely across the Italian Alps with his elephants when Macedonia initiated war with Rome. By the first century BC, the conquered province of Macedonia represented the edge of the

Roman Empire, serving as a buffer region to Asia Minor and the 'barbarian' tribes of Parthia, as well as the front of a new conflict with a deadly Roman foe to the east.

King Mithridates and his Kingdom of Pontus had challenged Roman imperialism for some four decades prior to Cato's tour of duty. Claiming direct descent from Alexander the Great along with Persian royalty, including Cyrus the Great and King Darius I, Mithridates was perhaps the most hated foreigner in Rome—loathed for having massacred an estimated eighty thousand Roman civilians in the year 88 BC. He had also spent years amassing an empire of his own, stretching his kingdom from the northern banks of the Black Sea to Armenia and into Syria. Some of Rome's greatest generals had been deployed to put down Mithridates in the field, and Macedonia was the natural staging area for this confrontation.

Cato was very cognizant of these troubling foreign affairs in the East, and the threat posed by the king dominated his year in Macedonia. With his privileged patrician name, Cato could have easily avoided such a hostile assignment. More than likely though, he specifically volunteered for the garrison in Macedonia, and the turbulent nature of the frontier post is added evidence of Cato's desire to build character on top of hard experience.

When he first greeted the troops of his legion, Cato did so from foot, having walked to Macedonia (while even his servants rode on horseback). Instead of barking orders or wielding corporal punishment to enforce his will, Cato was said to have always reasoned with his men, explaining what he wanted accomplished and why, and then bearing the burden of any chore with them. Afterwards, the legionaries were judged by their Stoic commander according to the merits of their performance.

Cato ate and slept in the trenches with his troops, marched by their side, and never asked anything he would not personally do himself. In this fashion, Plutarch epitomized Cato as the ideal 'man's man,' the model leader by example:

> For he willingly shared the tasks which he imposed upon others, and in his dress, way of living, and conduct on the march, made himself more like a soldier than a commander, while in character, dignity of purpose, and eloquence, he surpassed all those who bore the titles of Imperator and General.

It was clear that Cato fully integrated his knowledge and value of Stoicism with the leadership of his troops; in a word, he continued to 'walk the walk.'

This approach to command was very different than other contemporary accounts, which stand in stark contrast to Cato's example, a fact that was not likely lost on his troops in Macedonia. Marcus Crassus, the affluent power-broker who crucified the rebel slaves under Spartacus, had also resurrected the old technique of decimation, a brutal method of discipline, whereby every tenth Roman soldier was executed in front of their comrades if the army failed to meet expectations on the battlefield.

Even more recently, poor and careless treatment of the military culminated in blowback against senior management, altering the events of history. Several legions stationed near Cato's outpost in Macedonia had done the unthinkable. Exhausted from the relentless pursuit of Mithridates and frustrated by the shortage of plunder during the campaign, troops under the command of Lucius Licinius Lucullus refused orders. Pushed to the breaking point, the cohorts disobeyed their top officers, creating a *de facto* strike—unruly conditions rarely seen in the ranks of Rome's regimented war machine. Nonetheless, the defiance turned out one of the most consequential mutinies in the Roman Army.

Lucullus, who would later marry Cato's sister, was a formidable commander with a successful track record that included several battlefield wins. For years, though, he had failed to gain a decisive victory over King Mithridates. Committed to a steady operation of siege warfare and slow attrition, Lucullus's strategy hinged on the discipline of his troops, which was typically taken for granted. The mass disobedience by his army caught him by surprise.

To deal with this insubordination, along with Mithridates, the forty-year thorn in Rome's eastern side, the Senate relieved Lucullus and replaced him with Gnaeus Pompeius Magnus— or Pompey the Great. Pompey had long been something of a rising star in Roman politics. He had recently demonstrated his talents arresting a network of pirates in the Mediterranean and had previously waged a successful campaign against guerrilla partisans in Roman Spain.

By this day, the common manner to raise one's profile was through military conquests, a fact of life that suited Pompey's inflated ego, for among other things, the aspiring social climber was an excellent showman (the 'great' usually attached to his name was the result of a marketing gimmick, conferred on a teenage Pompey after an unimpressive military assignment).

Pompey had a knack for turning small achievements into the grandest of accomplishments, which sometimes entailed taking credit for the work of others. He arrived on the scene at the very close of the slave insurrection only to have word sent to Rome that he, not Crassus, had beaten Spartacus. And though Lucullus never finished off Mithridates, before he was relieved, he had laid waste to the king's army in a pivotal battlefield victory. Left with little more than a mopping-up operation, Pompey later presented himself as Rome's savior and champion, infuriating Lucullus, who would deride Pompey as a 'vulture' for feeding off the fame of others.

Lucullus, who was widely considered at the time to be Rome's finest general, had good reason to be heated, as Pompey's drive for public praise often dominated his judgment. So pervasive was his opportunism, his own paid insiders instigated the mutiny in Lucullus's legions, handing Pompey the chance to come to Rome's rescue. Not only did he make quick work of Mithridates's now-depleted rabble (according to the ancient scholar Appian, the king took his own life after his closest allies turned on him), but Pompey also made certain the whole Roman world knew of his 'great' feats. After further military campaigning in the Middle East, Pompey the Great gained for himself a flamboyant homecoming parade upon his return to the Senate.

In spite of the mayhem nearby, Cato and his troops saw no major combat in Macedonia, but as he completed his military commission, Cato's legionaries treated him like a conquering general. More than parades or medals, Cato was returning to Rome with the respect of his men, for throughout his entire command, he endured the harsh life of a soldier, alongside the very soldiers he led. Still a greater treasure for Cato was his new tutor, the Stoic philosopher Athenodorus—an educated man of high repute, who had been persuaded by Cato to accompany him home and assist with his continued studies.

Cato's homecoming

Cato returned to Rome and would soon enter public life in the Forum, the political center of the Republic. Only a few years had passed since Cato had been on the stump, campaigning alone for military tribune, but matters were rapidly changing. Since his time in the army, Roman politics was shifting in a direction that would prove fatal for republican governance. The Stoic war veteran sensed disaster on the horizon, and though others may have as well, few would be as alarmed as Cato.

Before Pompey left to deal the final blow to Mithridates, the ambitious prima donna had teamed up with Crassus shortly after the Spartacan scare was eliminated. Parking their respective armies outside the city walls, these competitors both ran and were elected as a political ticket for consul, the two highest positions in Rome. Marcus Crassus had an understandably low opinion of his colleague, for Pompey had done to him over the Spartacus affair what he later did to Lucullus over the campaign against King Mithridates—steal the show, and unduly hoard the credit. Annoyed with Pompey's preeminence, after someone announced that Pompey the Great was approaching, Crassus once retorted, 'As great as what?' Because of this distrust, both men refused to disband their armies, each blaming the other for their huge encampments situated on the outskirts of the city, effectively causing the election for the year 70 BC to be conducted at sword point.

The animosity between the two consul-elects actually predated this turn of events by nearly two decades, as did the Republic's mounting troubles. Pompey and Crassus were parties to a constitutional crisis that befell the Italian peninsula during the days of Cato's youth. In fact, many of the leading figures of the late Roman Republic had a hand in this most anti-republican experience—the dictatorship of one man: Lucius Cornelius Sulla.

A natural leader, Sulla had won a string of victories both on the battlefield and off. He was elected to the consulship, a rare achievement among his peers, given that the Senate consisted of hundreds of members, a fraction of which were ever lucky enough to gain the highest office in their lifetimes. And in northern Italy, he had also been credited with the pivotal defeat of a numerically-superior invasion force of Germanic and Celtic tribes.

Senior lieutenants in Sulla's army, both Pompey and Crassus, along with Lucullus, stood behind the gifted military tactician while he swiftly rose to power, in what would be a messy civil war. As Sulla's influence elevated, so did the partisan prospects of his loyal underlings. At the close of the year 88 BC, a chaotic chapter from Roman history opened, one that witnessed a brief but bloody autocracy within the capital, establishing a dangerous precedent for the next generation.

By the time of Sulla's bloodletting, the permanent legions throughout Rome's provinces were now only as loyal to the elected officials in Rome as their general was; their compensation owed, not from the Senate, but from their commanding officer's distribution of loot from their constant campaigns. With the property qualification done away with by the recent reforms to the army, the average Roman warrior no longer held land at home. Home was the army itself. The mission, albeit unofficially, had transformed from the defense of Roman-held property to the conquest of new property for the Roman soldier. Only a fragile connection linked the soldiers in the field with the Senate's authority in the capital, and this was the Senate's ability to appoint the army's leaders. If this formal ability broke down—for instance, if a provincial governor simply refused to relinquish command to a new Senate appointee—then so too did the army's obedience to the Roman political body (one main reason why a future Cato in the Senate would be skeptical of personal ambition with the men chosen to head the legions in the provinces).

Beyond these deeply destabilizing political forces, on the surface, the Sullan dilemma started over King Mithridates and his upstart trouble-making on the frontier. Much younger in Sulla's day and in the prime of his war-fighting ability, Mithridates had posed a serious menace. To solve the predicament, the Senate initially dispatched Sulla to take command of Rome's eastern armies, only to issue a decree shortly thereafter, reneging on the decision, replacing Sulla with his former boss, Gaius Marius—the man ironically responsible for the reorganization of the military.

Behind the scenes, Marius had lobbied the Senate to change its mind, more than likely because the populist reformer resented his protégé's success. Sulla was not only regarded as Rome's most capable general, he was also the elected consul. The law in this matter was clearly on his side: whenever hostile forces materialized, constitutional tradition had always charged the consuls with leading Rome's armies. To further complicate matters, Marius was a private citizen at the time, and no longer eligible for command. The Senate's decision to swap Sulla with Marius at the head of the army was more than just a public insult; it was illegal.

Not to be outdone, Sulla would prove his legions exclusively answered to him. Forbidden for centuries in Roman society, Sulla did what no general had done since the birth of the Republic, over four hundred years earlier: he ordered his army into the capital city. What began as a peripheral conflict in the East quickly escalated to internal violence on the streets of Rome. Easily overcoming Marius's factions, Sulla seized power for himself. By the end of the decade, Sulla had reinstated the Roman dictatorship, and even though his autocracy lasted for just one year, it was a time of havoc for the Roman ruling class. To eliminate opposition, and fundraise at the same time, Sulla implemented his proscriptions. Long lists of his political enemies were posted in the Forum, authorizing the execution of the individuals named. Bounties were granted to the killers, while the victims of the purging had their estates sold, the property awarded to the highest bidder.

Fortunes were made hunting down Sulla's 'dead men walking.' Irrespective of the dictator's political agenda, the friends and supporters of the new regime murdered their own competitors and seized their property—only to have the names of the dead added to the official hit-lists afterwards. Through this perverted enterprise, Marcus Crassus, Pompey's envious peer, began amassing his personal wealth in the slaughterhouse that was Sulla's court.

The scale of the bloodletting was unprecedented. The ancient Greek-born historian Cassius Dio recounted that Sulla topped his rivals in all things, even atrocities: 'A certain longing came over him to go far beyond all others in the variety also of his murders, as if there were some virtue in being excelled by none, even in blood-guiltiness.' By the time the terror ended, as many as nine thousand Roman citizens had been eradicated via Sulla's despotic decrees.

Just a boy during Sulla's reign, Cato and his aristocratic siblings were expected to make social calls at the dictator's request.

After one such visit, the Stoic in training purportedly asked his babysitter why nothing was done about such tyranny. 'Because my child, men fear him more than they hate him,' to which Cato replied, 'Why then, do you not give me a sword—that I might kill him and set my country free from slavery?'

In spite of the atrocities, Sulla likely had good intentions, insomuch as the republican cause was concerned. This much was underscored by his voluntary abdication of power (something a future dictator, one Julius Caesar, would call Sulla's biggest mistake). As quickly as Sulla gained absolute authority, he gave it back. He put into motion several reforms, all aimed at strengthening the supremacy of the Senate—which in his mind, would prevent future chaos and restore constitutional law, even with the character of standing armies intact. On his retirement from public life, shortly before his death in 78 BC, Sulla believed his power-grab saved the Republic. He was wrong. Instead of saving the State, Sulla simply provided a new way to replace it.

The damage had a lasting effect, outliving Sulla through his apprentices, who looked upon him as a political trailblazer. His two impressionable fans, Pompey and Crassus, both learned by his example that violence was not just the 'continuation of politics by other means.' In their post-Sullan world, violence *was* politics.

When he began his public life, Cato was all too familiar with the decline of constitutional rule. In his teenage years, Cato witnessed the carnage of Sulla's proscriptions firsthand. He also knew the power unscrupulous men like Pompey and Crassus could wield in the Forum, under the close scepter of their illegal armies. Cato was determined to right the ship. Committed to republican values, which he equated with Roman *libertas*, Cato represented uncompromising virtue and a sincere dedication to constitutional tradition to his contemporaries. Though his opponents may have denigrated his conservative views, and at times his methods, they never questioned Cato's honesty—or his resolve. These distinguishing traits soon made clear to his colleagues, restoring the Republic was Cato's *raison d'être.*

Assuming public office

In 65 BC, at the age of thirty, Cato was elected to the office of quaestor. The lowest-ranking position of the three major categories making up the Senate (below the senatorial grades of praetor and consul), the twenty quaestors were responsible for the maintenance of financial records and general accounting of the Roman treasury. They also served as aides to the two consuls, the dual chief executives of the State. For any other up-and-coming politician, it was dull work. Cato though would make all he could out of the position, lending so much gravity to its duties, he postponed running for the spot until he was confident he understood all the particulars.

For some time, the quaestors had been at the center of the corruption that characterized Roman politics. Although they were at the bottom of the hierarchy within the Senate, they were the sole gatekeepers to public funds. Bribery of quaestors was considered custom. Graft and embezzlement in the Roman 'department of the treasury' was just a routine part of the job.

Prevailing social norms of iniquity made the quaestorship more about being a clever bookie than a good accountant. With seedy financial shenanigans, they frequently padded their own wallets and lined the pockets of their aristocratic friends—all by pilfering the public coffer.

Making the bully pulpit of his new position bigger than what it had ever been, Cato launched a blistering crusade against this institutionalized racket. He fired loads of bureaucrats and indicted those he judged guilty of shirking the law. Even when the jury had, in one case, exonerated a senior clerk accused of taking kickbacks, Cato refused to reinstate the man, making it clear he intended to clean house.

He also reconciled the State's finances, which as a consequence of incompetence or corruption, had been egregiously mismanaged. Combing through legal records, Cato settled outstanding accounts that were genuinely owed to creditors, while compelling payment in full from debtors who were under the impression they had skirted their responsibility of reimbursing loans received.

The boldest action the maturing Stoic undertook, though, was his decision to right the wrongs from Sulla's proscriptions. Cato prosecuted individuals who had participated in the dictator's headhunting, bringing justice on those who looted and murdered their fellow Romans marked to die during Sulla's bloodbath.

Some of these men were Cato's fellow senators, living high on the hog from property and capital they had accrued hacking to death Sulla's targets. Throughout the dictatorship, the bounties awarded to Sulla's many hitmen were paid out from the Roman treasury. This element of state-financing behind Sulla's purge allowed Cato, in his station of watchdog over the public's money, to assert a legal argument for his day of reckoning. Some fifteen years after the purges, Cato confronted the men who were guilty, demanded the blood money be refunded, and charged them with murder. Handing them over to the courts, scores of Sulla's former culprits were convicted and sentenced to death.

Without a doubt, Cato's brazen conduct made him plenty of enemies during his term as quaestor. In spite of the political blowback, his authentic appeal won him general acclaim from Roman society, along with respect from many of his colleagues who quietly agreed with his actions. In fact, his name became a figure of speech in his own day. 'I won't believe it, even if Cato says it's true' became an expression used in everyday conversation, a testament to Cato's character.

Cato takes on corruption

Cato's struggle to make Rome honest again was an uphill battle, for growing corruption within a bloated bureaucracy was a mere symptom of a deeper illness. Over the previous decades, money and tribute had poured into the public treasury from the new territories subjugated by Roman military conquest. By replacing landowners with the more numerous landowner-wannabe's, the army had solved its manpower shortage, but more significantly, the spreading empire was equipped with the capability to continue its expansion. However, the increased plunder from subduing more provinces led to fierce political infighting, over just who would control this immense redistribution of wealth.

Reorganizing the army with plebeians was not simply a utilitarian solution to a recruitment problem; it was a populist political move. A new constituency had been realized. Cut the poor plebs in on the loot—secure them paid positions in the army, or better yet, the promise of free grain and the termination of their debts—and with the support of the masses, one could bypass the established aristocracy altogether along the road to power.

Drawing from this grassroots base at their disposal, radical populists emerged throughout Roman political circles, beginning with the Gracchi brothers in the late second century BC. In the fashion of Marius, Sulla's former army mentor, the *populares* faction of Roman politics agitated for policies designed to appease the bottom ranks of Roman society. Their domestic agenda included subsidized grain, land redistribution, and debt relief. Ostensibly these were tailored to aid the commoners, but a self-serving agenda always existed, particularly when such measures would help rally large swaths of the population, bestowing populist-partisans with extraordinary influence.

A major consequence from this 'progressive' movement is that violence increasingly became standard practice in Roman politics (on full display with the armies of Pompey and Crassus, during their election to consul). Tiberius Gracchus, the original star of the *populares*, was assassinated during a riot in the year 133 BC for promoting the confiscation of land from nobles in order to award the real estate to his plebeian constituency (a decade later, his younger brother Gaius was forced to commit suicide for advocating the same scheme). Fifty years after this groundwork, while Sulla was away campaigning in the East,

Marius, the populist military reformer, seized his chance in Rome, systematically wiping out conservative politicians in ways that rivaled Sulla's brutality. Where they had failed, though, the next generation of *populares* would not.

One such demagogue attempted to take this political violence to new heights. Instead of using violence to achieve certain ends within the Roman state, Catiline colluded with his populist allies to overthrow the entire state apparatus. A former partisan of Sulla's, Catiline allegedly killed his own brother, adding his name to the proscription list afterwards to excuse the fratricide.

Now endeavoring to imitate Sulla, Catiline plotted to assassinate Roman senators in their homes. With an army of disgruntled war veterans at his back, who felt they had been shafted with their retirement packages, Catiline's plan was to march on Rome and claim power for himself. The whole affair unraveled over the course of the year 63 BC, when the consulship was occupied by the one Roman who today, the very most is known about from his own hand.

Marcus Tullius Cicero had journeyed 'the road less traveled' on his climb to consul. An outstanding orator, Cicero reached high office, not through military exploits, but as a criminal defense attorney. As a 'new man' without patrician ancestors, this achievement is all the more remarkable. His rhetorical skills in court grew his fame and won him many clients, but Cicero was more than just a gifted speaker.

During his youth, Cicero studied philosophy in Greece, under the leading intellectuals of the day, including Posidonius of Rhodes, one of the most revered theorists of the Stoic school. Cicero became a brilliant thinker in his own right, developing key ideas on natural law and political theory. Many of the towering figures of Western civilization were profoundly influenced by the Roman lawyer; St. Augustine, John Locke, and Thomas Jefferson were admitted 'Ciceronians.'

Few have ever surpassed his ability as a writer. Cicero's extensive scholarship consisted of several treatises in political science and many more pieces on ethics. By his Latin prose, one of his lasting contributions was bringing Greek philosophy to the Roman world, transmitting through the centuries crucial Western principles to later Medieval Europe. Much of Cicero's collective work still survives, alongside hundreds of his personal letters.

Though he was not a self-identified Stoic, Cicero was sympathetic to the philosophy. This was especially true toward the end of his life, when his desire for personal ambition and political neutrality faded—and his admiration for Cato and his virtuous example had grown.

In his own time, Cicero was one of the few who understood that the Republic's problems were larger than a simple clash of personalities. As the empire expanded, deep structural cracks became wider and more defective. The violence and civil wars were byproducts of Rome's perpetual foreign conflict: the State had sanctioned conquest as a way of life. 'A war which is launched without provocation cannot possibly be just,' Cicero once reflected. But more than this, he also abhorred Rome's militant regime *in toto*:

> It is a hard thing to say, but we Romans are loathed abroad because of the damage our generals and officials have done in their licentiousness. No temple has been protected by its sanctity, no state

by its sworn agreements, no house and home by
its locks and bars—in fact, there is now a shortage
of prosperous cities for us to declare war on so
that we can loot them afterwards. Do you think
that when we send out an army against an enemy
it is to protect our allies, or is it rather to use the
war as an excuse for plundering them? Do you
know of a single state that we have subdued that
is still rich, or a single rich state that our generals
have not subdued?

Cicero recognized the inherent pitfalls of the world's first military
industrial complex, an immoral policy that threatened to undo
the Republic.

Initially, the propaganda from the populist crowd was but
a small-minded nuisance for Cicero, another side effect from
empire building. But it was an annoyance that steadily escalated
with the growth of Roman conquest. Eventually, Cicero would
reach Cato's conclusion, that the *populares* were more than just
rabble-rousers. They held seditious designs for the capture of
state power, a serious danger that had to be confronted.

Catiline's attempted *coup d'état* solidified this opinion. But
towards the end of the 60's BC, Cicero was enjoying his early
political victories. Cautious and overly sensitive to making
waves, he often proved very indecisive. Cicero's success through
the ordeal would require help from the most outspoken member
of the *optimates*, the conservative faction of the Roman Senate.

The rise of Julius Caesar

With Cicero's consulship, respect for Cato was concretely established, especially within the cluster of 'better men' which opposed the *populares*—and at the time, also predominated the Senate in numbers. Catiline's conspiracy, though, pitted the Stoic icon against a man who would become his archenemy for the rest of his life: Gaius Julius Caesar.

Five years older than Cato, Caesar was his polar opposite. Unlike Cato, Caesar was descended from an ancient family of rich patrician ancestry, though he was anything but traditional. The level of Cato's austerity was equaled by Caesar's taste for extravagance, in both his private and public affairs. A notorious womanizer, Caesar showed very little self-control in his personal exploits. He was also obsessed with appearances, taking pains to show off trend-setting fashions, and cultured dress. Caesar's elections were secured through bribery, as were many of his legal cases where he presided as magistrate. While Cato saw virtue as an ultimate end, Caesar lusted for glory. According to Plutarch, after his friends caught him in tears reading through Alexander the Great's adventures, Caesar is said to have remarked: 'Do you not think it is matter for sorrow that while Alexander, at my age, was already king of so many peoples, I have as yet achieved no brilliant success?'

A nephew to Marius, Caesar was by family and social circles, a natural member of the *populares* bloc. After the defeat of his uncle's followers, he fled Rome during Sulla's rule, in order to escape the reprisals against the populists. However, Caesar's maternal family, who had been long-time party faithfuls to Sulla, successfully interceded on his behalf. The imperial biographer Suetonius later related the dictator's forewarning:

> Very well then, you win! Take him! But never
> forget that the man whom you want me to spare
> will one day prove the ruin of the party which
> you and I have so long defended. There are many
> Marius's in this fellow Caesar.

Even so, Caesar joined the army, returning to Rome only after Sulla had relinquished power. Impoverished by Sulla's repossession of his inheritance, Caesar racked up immense debts in order to forward his political career. In a twist of satire, his chief creditor came to be Marcus Crassus, Sulla's crony who profited from the purges, becoming a multimillionaire off the same mode which landed Caesar in the poorhouse. Regardless, the relationship would prove indispensable to Caesar, who pinned much of his early career hopes on excessive campaign spending.

In the wake of Sulla's murders, a leadership vacuum arose within the ranks of the *populares*. Two decades after Marius's death, Caesar was jockeying to fill his late uncle's shoes. He had been a good soldier away from home, winning the Civic Crown for gallantry in battle, the Roman equivalent to the Medal of Honor. In 65 BC, Caesar was elected to the office of aedile, which duties included supervising the grain supply and, conveniently for a populist, managing public entertainment. While Cato the quaestor was upsetting the establishment, Caesar the aedile was busy showering the crowds with lavish games and gladiator matches. By the time the pandemonium from Catiline arrived, Crassus's investment was paying off: Caesar's stock was on the rise.

Classical historians offer some evidence which incriminates Caesar in Catiline's plot. Prior to the conspiracy, Caesar, along with Crassus, had openly backed Catiline against Cicero for the consulship. This is unsurprising given Caesar's up-and-coming status within the populist faction of Roman politics. Crassus on the other hand, aimed to construct a block of allies in order to curtail Pompey's forthcoming celebrity status upon his rival's inevitable return from the eastern military campaign. Bankrolling IOU's was one way to make loyal friends.

But putting their man in office is quite different than overthrowing the existing order. It is unlikely that Caesar would have risked alienating himself from the Roman aristocracy, on the meager prospects of a renegade and a rabble force of elderly ex-soldiers (even if Catiline was proven successful, Caesar would have already garnered favor from his earlier support of the fanatic's losing bid for the consulship).

What stands as more improbable is that Caesar's financier, one of the wealthiest Romans in the money-lending business, would have thrown 'all in' with a person who was serious about universal debt cancellation, as Catiline had so vowed. Crassus desired political access and fame, not revolution and uncertainty. Though the sources are generally inconclusive, neither man was a likely candidate for Catiline's hasty, ill-fated insurrection.

Cato confronts Caesar

The situation came to a boiling point late in 63 BC, after Catiline had lost his second consecutive election for the consulship earlier in the year. With the constitutional avenues to high power closed to him, he left the city to raise an army.

He did so under extreme suspicion, as his conspiracy was more than just rumor mill by the time he slipped town. Cicero as consul, and thus head of state, had been continually fed information by informants as the plot progressed. Having soundly beaten Catiline in the election a year before, he was wary of his former competitor, paranoid of the lengths a sore loser might be willing to undertake. After receiving detailed intelligence on the final stages of the plot, including written communication between the conspirators, along with uncovering a large stockpile of weapons hidden away in one of their homes, Cicero convened the Senate.

In a series of meetings, Cicero blasted Catiline and his band of followers, just as he had all year. His colleagues in the Senate had grown accustomed to his exaggerated rhetoric, but with the new evidence Cicero presented, many began to feel the gravity of the developing danger. This was especially the case once it was learned that Catiline and his accomplices intended to recruit slaves to their mutiny, no doubt bringing back horror stories of Spartacus and the uprising which had wiped out several Roman armies.

Catiline was branded an enemy of the State, and the leading collaborators, who had evidently remained in Rome to carry out the assassinations, were placed under arrest. The question now before the Senate was what to do with the captives. Traditionally, Roman citizens were not subject to capital punishment without trial, but this was no ordinary crime. This was sedition, in the most heinous degree.

Catiline's armies were gathering in small villages outside Rome, and the threat to the Roman state was perceived as dire. To deal with the crisis, the Senate had voted to give emergency powers to the consul. As such, Cicero already had the authority to execute the conspirators, without even asking for the Senate's permission.

Like Cato, Cicero had lived through terrible times and sought to prevent the type of wholesale political upheaval another Sulla or Marius could bring. What's more is that Catiline and his henchmen had personally targeted Cicero for elimination, a fact never lost on the orator. In less than a month, though, Cicero's term as consul would end, and with it, the legal insulation that his office afforded—leaving him open to prosecution, should any aggrieved friends or family members of the prisoners wish to pursue charges in court. Though Cicero favored the death penalty, he moved with characteristic caution. To avoid taking sole blame for the decision, either way it went, he decided to put the matter to a vote.

One by one the senators voiced their support for the 'extreme penalty.' It appeared as if there would be no dispute until Julius Caesar rose to address the assembly. Arguing against the death penalty, Caesar spoke firmly in favor of house arrest, that the accused men should be detained until they stood trial at some point in the future, presumably after the crisis passed. Acquiescing to Caesar, the mood of the body turned. Senators who had previously called for death, shifted their positions to support Caesar's wish of imprisonment.

It was a clever move. On its face, it seemed that Caesar had provided a level-headed response, urging restraint and prudence. His speech even emphasized the establishment of poor legal precedent; that while they should not fear Cicero, another consul in the future may abuse such power. However, strategy in the long term probably explains Caesar's real motive. All of the men involved in the plot were populists, which at the time, were in short order in the Senate. The ranks of the *populares* had been severely depleted with Sulla's purges, and Caesar needed all the political backing of his faction he could get going forward if he was to prevent his own career from stalling. At minimum, he had to act like he cared about the outcome of his populist conspirators, just to satisfy the base.

Cato was appalled. To him, the highest crime was blatant ruin of sacred law. In this respect, Caesar's call was not for upholding Rome's constitution, but for willfully ignoring its defense. There was no virtue in weakness; duty called for strength. A message had to be sent to Catiline, his mob of followers in the field, and those who may try subversion in the future: the Senate would not tolerate traitors. For Cato, treason was a capital offense. And it was not simply a utilitarian matter; justice in the abstract sense required a proportional penance.

Cato was also intimately aware of how easy it was for Catiline in particular to escape this justice. The populist was one of the many cronies Cato as quaestor had brought up on charges for partaking in Sulla's proscriptions. At trial, Catiline was acquitted, likely because the court had been bribed, owed to Catiline's deep family connections. And the Roman who presided as judge over Catiline's trial: Julius Caesar.

While his oratory lacked Cicero's lofty style, Cato was a solid speaker. He never rehearsed his speeches, which, combined with his command of the material, enabled him to remain both authentic and direct. He also possessed the uncanny ability to speak from sunup to sundown, and he often did in the Senate, to forestall unconstitutional legislation. Much to the annoyance of his enemies, Cato invented the filibuster.

On this occasion, Cato addressed his colleagues in a harsh tone. As the debate over the fate of Catiline's conspirators fell to him, he called out those who had flip-flopped and challenged the commitment of his fellow senators, both to Rome and its heritage. The collaborators had confessed. The matter was no longer about guilt or innocence. And trial? To Cato, the very deliberation they were undergoing in the Senate was in fact the trial.

But he reserved the roughest treatment for Caesar. By advising mercy, Cato accused Caesar of aiding and abetting villains, who by their own admission were guilty of the most sinister actions. Already mistrusted for his political support of Catiline in the past, Caesar's benevolence was a mere charade to Cato. The Stoic would not allow such disingenuous overtures to stand. Plutarch recorded Cato's reprimand, which reminded Caesar and the rest of the Senate where their sympathies should lie:

> Caesar, he said, under a popular pretext and with humane words, was trying to subvert the state; he was seeking to frighten the senate in a case where he himself had much to fear; and he might be well content if he should come off guiltless of what had been done and free from suspicion, since he was so openly and recklessly trying to rescue the common enemies, while for his country, which had been on the brink of ruin, and was so good and great, he confessed that he had no pity; and yet for men who ought not to have lived or been born even, he was shedding tears and lamenting, although by their deaths they would free the state from great slaughter and perils.

By the time Cato finished, his speech was met with enthusiastic applause. Cicero signaled for the vote, and the motion for capital punishment carried. Not only did Cato win the day, but he demonstrated in dramatic fashion that he was a force to be reckoned with.

———◆———

Courage over compromise

The commotion from Catiline's affair did not end with the executions of the conspirators. Catiline's army was still in the field, and in light of the potential threat, some of Pompey's backers saw an opportunity in the aftermath of the Senate's crisis.

Metellus Nepos, a loyalist to Pompey, devised a plan. Under the pretext of Rome's savior, Pompey would be called back from the East to secure the city with his armies. Nepos, in his position as tribune, would take such a proposal straight to a people's assembly. If ratified, the resolution would be passed into law, irrespective of the Senate's consent.

Cato quite possibly viewed Pompey's army as the more dangerous of the two, for Catiline's force was not only weak, but it lacked legitimacy. Pompey's legions were an entirely different matter. Though a tribune could bypass the Senate with legislation, another tribune was vested with the constitutional authority to veto such actions. At the turn of the year 62 BC, Cato had also been elected tribune alongside Metellus Nepos, who answered his colleague's plan with a pledge, 'that while he lived, Pompey should not enter the city with an armed force.'

Before Metellus Nepos could test Cato's resolve, Catiline's ragtag militia crumbled. Upon hearing the news of the fate of their ringleaders inside Rome, most of Catiline's army deserted in panic, while the leftovers were easily put down in quick action (Catiline himself was killed in the decisive battle). With the threat dissolved, Pompey's tribune forfeited the effort to pass his law. Cato's republicans had withstood populist conspiracy, but populist politics was far from over.

Catiline or no Catiline, Pompey was coming back to Rome. Though his supporters had failed at their attempts to make him the next Sulla by law, King Mithridates was dead and the eastern frontier finally settled. Pompey would demand respect for such a performance; his oversized ego asked for nothing less. With the next election for consul just months away, Pompey the Great could make an entrance with an even bigger splash.

To qualify for the ballot, Roman law obligated candidates for public office to be personally present at the time of their election. Travel was slow for the smallest of caravans in the first century BC, and Pompey was managing a long route at the head of many legions. Further complicating Pompey's plans, victorious generals were legally entitled to a homecoming parade, or a triumph, but only after their armies were disbanded. Even if Pompey made Rome in time for the election, he would be forced to disperse his army and forego his triumph—if he was to enter the city and compete as a candidate.

This choice may seem immaterial, but a Roman triumph was no ordinary celebration. The exposure that came with such an over-the-top spectacle was an invaluable source of power in itself. To a man like Pompey, who craved public affection, it was everything.

Of course, the core of the matter was Pompey's army. If the election law could be changed, the conditions Pompey's supporters had sought to bring about in the wake of Catiline's conspiracy could be replicated, yet with even better results. As an elected consul with a loyal army intact, Pompey could simply arrive in Rome, enjoy his welcoming parade, and achieve supreme power with a legitimacy that averted any admission to it. For Pompey to have his cake and eat it too, Metellus Nepos would have to offer another proposal, this one permitting the returning war hero to stand for election *in absentia*.

If Pompey's name was added to the ballot, he was a shoo-in for the consulship—and Cato knew it. Pompey was favored by the crowds, especially since his loyal cadre in Rome had taken care to promote his status as Rome's protector, while he was gone in the East. But his supporters had also successfully solicited the aid of Julius Caesar, who saw an opening to redeem himself after his humiliating defeat in the Senate over Catiline's conspiracy. By tying himself to Pompey, the leader of the *populares* could ride the coattails of his public adoration, while at the same time, hand Cato a setback of his own.

Cato was determined to block Nepos's new law. Relinquishing an army to run for office was a deep-seated Roman principle, on par with the American legal standard under the Posse Comitatus Act. The presence of the candidate in the city ahead of the election helped maintain the practice of civilian control. Pompey had already managed to keep his army mobilized once during an election, in his first consulship with Crassus. Less than a decade had passed since the excuse of his co-consul's army, together with the fear of King Mithridates in the East, had lent Pompey the political cover he needed to duck tradition. Cato would not run the risk of martial law a second time.

The ability to circumvent the Senate, combined with the useful element of demagoguery, would make public assemblies a hallmark of the *populares*. These open meetings in the Forum could be a deadly business though. With high unemployment and the swelling acceptance of the welfare state, social unrest had become a routine part of city life. At a moment's notice, tension at political rallies often sparked riots. The night before Nepos was to propose his law, Cato's friends and family pleaded with him not to attend. Though many other senators were opposed to Nepos's measure, Cato would be the only one making a stern effort to stop it. To do so, he would have to make his way through a hostile audience, navigate past enemies allied to the *populares*, struggle towards the podium, and formally pronounce to the gathering his veto of the legislation.

Undaunted by concerns from his inner circle, the Stoic dutifully arrived on scene early the next morning, focused on the one task within his control as tribune. Nepos was perched on a stage overlooking the crowd. Seated next to him was Julius Caesar. Armed guards had been stationed on the steps leading to their position, the mob in attendance packed tight with Pompey's partisans and Caesar's hired thugs.

The proceeding had started by the time Cato forged ahead, loudly announcing his presence to the assembly's two leaders: 'What a bold man—and what a coward—to levy such an army against a single unarmed and defenseless person!' Accompanied only by a few brave friends, the guards briefly parted for Cato, doubtlessly put off by his show of tenacity. A clerk had already begun to read the resolution, as Cato ascended the stairs, plopped himself down between Nepos and Caesar, and interrupted the process with his cries of 'veto!'

The clerk's presentation now broken up, Nepos grabbed the resolution himself. In desperation, he attempted to personally read the document. Cato responded by quickly snatching it from his hands. When Nepos next tried to recite it from memory, Cato's friend, who had followed his fearless colleague up to the podium, reached out with his hand and forced the tribune's mouth shut.

Chaos ensued as fighting erupted in the crowd. Nepos ordered his armed guards to rush the podium. Firmly committed to his veto, Cato found himself at one point alone on stage, dodging a barrage of rocks hurled at him by a horde of plebs loyal to Caesar. Cato's steel backbone, though, emboldened the conservative base who, in a show of support, managed to push to the front of the gathering. Caesar had retreated in the melee, and with the momentum clearly in Cato's favor—and realizing 'that his followers were completely terrified before Cato and thought him utterly invincible'—Metellus Nepos finally withdrew as well.

Cato followed up his veto victory with another one in the Senate. Becoming something of a majority leader, Cato pressed his conservative *optimates* to pass a resolution condemning Pompey's attempt to change the election law for his own interest. Realizing the political order in Rome was positioned against him, Pompey changed his tact, disbanding his army to return as a lobbyist.

His agenda consisted of new lands for his veterans, as Pompey had promised his faithful constituency, as well as the reorganization of the eastern provinces he had conquered after his defeat of Mithridates (no doubt to enrich himself with his cut of the taxes). Last but certainly not least, Pompey wanted his triumph. With the exception of the latter, which Pompey eventually celebrated down the streets of Rome in spectacular arrangement, the Stoic leading the statehouse thwarted the conqueror at every turn, using his now-perfected filibuster to kill the populist legislation. With little room to maneuver, Pompey would try a new approach. Unaccustomed to defeat, Pompey resorted to a strategy of joining his enemy, rather than beating him. Recently divorced, he offered to marry Cato's daughter. Marriage alliances were a cultural norm in Roman politics, but Cato considered such a deal a compromise to his integrity. He rejected Pompey's proposal out of hand.

Many historians, Plutarch included, have been hard on Cato for what they see as a stubborn dismissal and attach blame for what happened in the years afterwards to his decision to turn away the wedding proposition, which inevitably pushed Pompey to ally with Caesar. However, Cato was deeply suspicious of his daughter's new suitor, and he had good reason to be. Pompey was, after all, a former loyalist to Sulla, the man who had nearly been the Republic's undoing. Pompey had also proven his willingness to use an army to achieve his political ambitions—as demonstrated by his first election to the consulship in 70 BC. Nearly a decade later, with more battlefield victories under his belt, and another procession to parade them about, Pompey's stature in the eyes of the Roman public had only skyrocketed. In the hands of a man who sought such things, glory and fame on this magnitude could translate into power of an equal size, and it is not difficult to picture the rationale behind the Stoic's distrust. In any event, Cato's rebuff backed Pompey into a corner.

The growing power of Caesar

In the year 60 BC, Caesar returned from Spain where, as the appointed governor, he had effectively waged an aggressive campaign against warring factions in the region. At the age of forty, Caesar was now eligible for the office of consul, and with the upcoming election, the ambitious praetor faced the same time-stricken dilemma Pompey had: enjoy a triumph for military success, or compete in the election by relinquishing his *imperium*, the right to command his provincial army in the field. Just as Pompey had done, Caesar would request an exemption to the law to have both.

If Cato had been suspicious of Pompey's long-term intentions, he most certainly was of Caesar's. Here was a man who not only represented vain disregard for Rome's conservative traditions, in both his populist rhetoric and chic appearance, but had backed Catiline for office, the seditious dissident who had made the most serious attempt to overthrow the Republic since Sulla. From dawn until dusk, Cato once again used the parliamentary rules of the Senate to ensure Caesar's special treatment was doomed. Unlike Pompey, though, Caesar's choice from the denial would sacrifice the triumph for a chance at high office.

Having solicited key supporters with personal letters while he was still in Spain, Caesar had lain the groundwork early. Along with financial backing from Crassus and other moneyed individuals who saw value in his rising star, Caesar cruised by the opposition to an easy election win. His immediate priority for his consulship during the year 59 BC was a land bill, which would establish a commission to dole out real estate for the urban poor, as well as veterans from the legions—the two powerful special-interest groups emerging as the political base for the *populares*.

Such a policy would prove more than difficult, and Caesar knew it. Cicero had not yet committed to supporting Caesar's agrarian law. As an ex-consul and hero of the Catiline affair, his opinion carried weight, especially when it was framed by his legendary rhetorical talents. But the crux of the matter was Cato, who had repeatedly confirmed his determination to halt the populist agenda. He had recently crushed similar land redistribution attempts from Pompey, and his refusal to entertain Caesar's election request foreshadowed a year of stiff opposition. If Caesar was to achieve any success as consul, he would need to find a way to sidestep the loud voice of the *optimates*.

A coalition emerged from Cato's resistance, or what the Roman historian Titus Livy styled 'a conspiracy against the state by its three leading citizens.' This informal pact between Caesar, Crassus, and Pompey would come to be known as the First Triumvirate, and though all of the major players had different objectives, they all had a common foe in one Marcus Porcius Cato.

Caesar likely brokered the *quid pro quo* arrangement, particularly considering he was the link between the two otherwise archrivals from an earlier era. Caesar had always thrown token support to Pompey's causes and had long garnered close ties to Crassus through the many elections bought with his flush colleague's bank account. Pompey had not made much political headway since his return from the East, while Crassus sought opportunity to equal Pompey's military exploits with a worthwhile provincial posting, as well as lucrative deals for his business interests. Caesar, as chief magistrate, was in a position to aid their ambition, so long as they assisted his. To do so, they would have to neutralize Cato.

———◆◆———

Cato's stand against the populists

Consideration in the Senate over Caesar's agrarian law began with no disapproval. As former consuls, Crassus and Pompey were privileged with speaking first. As can be expected, the two members of the new three-pronged alliance endorsed the bill that would finally award Pompey's veterans their promised lands. Others held their tongue, no doubt intimidated by the powerful trifecta now directing the Senate House. Yet the trouble did not start until the debate came to Cato, who stood and explained that while the bill was not terribly crafted, major reforms should be postponed until a later time. Cato kept talking and showed no signs of letting up, making it clear he intended to prevent a vote through another feat of endurance. Frustrated and angry at the man who so often had made him look foolish, Caesar had him arrested.

By throwing Cato in jail, though, Caesar committed a major misstep. The Senate was still stacked with men like Publicola, Cato's former army commander, who once praised the Stoic for his gallant service during the conflict against Spartacus. Or it comprised senators like Lucullus, who had married Cato's sister and, in the near past, gladly assisted with the obstruction of proposals from Pompey, the man who at one time helped provoke a mutiny among Lucullus's legions, sabotaging his command against Mithridates in the East.

As Cato was hauled off by Caesar's guards, many rank and file members of the *optimates* began to abruptly leave the Senate House in disgust. When Caesar asked one such senator where he was headed, Cassius Dio noted the reply: 'I would rather be in prison with Cato, than here in the Senate with you.' The arrest and the subsequent protest had the same effect as Cato's filibuster. No vote was taken on Caesar's land bill, while the backlash forced the consul to release Cato. Once again, the Stoic had proven an obstacle to Caesar.

Cato's gain, though, was short-lived. Within days, Caesar sidestepped the Senate and, as he had before with Metellus Nepos, took his bill straight to a public assembly for ratification. This time, however, he had the popular Pompey with him who, along with Crassus, peddled the welfare programs to the crowd. Cato arrived on the scene with his son-in-law, Marcus Bibulus, the other consul serving in office that year alongside Caesar.

With their small group of supporters, the same tactics that were used to avert Pompey's election bill were repeated—but with very different results. Caesar had learned from the mistakes of the past, and with thousands of Pompey's veterans in the crowd, many of whom were well-armed, the odds arrayed against Cato were too overwhelming. Bibulus was pelted by the masses and forced to retreat, but not before a bucket of manure was dumped over his back. Cato was the last of the tiny group to leave. Weathering the insults and projectiles from an angry mob friendly to the Triumvirate, he remained near the stage in a futile attempt to stop the proceeding, finally retiring from the gathering just before the bill was passed by majority vote.

Caesar scored major points, but perhaps more significantly, the leader of the *populares* made it known that though Cato might have sway in the Senate House, he had control of the crowds. Adding insult to injury, a clause in the bill stipulated that every senator must take an oath, swearing to uphold the new law and never seek its repeal, something Caesar likely viewed as an added sweetener. Upon hearing of Cato's plans to accept exile rather than pledge Caesar's cronyism, Cicero pleaded with him to reconsider and, according to Plutarch, appealed to the Stoic's sense of duty: 'for even if Cato did not need his country, his country needed Cato.' Begrudgingly, Cato took his friend's advice, becoming the last senator to receive the mandated oath.

As the welfare state is prone to expansion, Caesar pushed for a second major agrarian law only months later. This time his bill's target was the redistribution of plush farm land in Campania, a wealthy region of aristocratically-held real estate outside the city, which had been exempt from the first land bill. By this time, opposition to Caesar had completely evaporated, either by way of bribery or through fear of the Triumvirate. Cato was the lone source of resistance, but in the short term, little could be done against Caesar's mastery of manipulating crowded public assemblies to implement his schemes. All Cato could do was protest, as the checks and traditions which had secured the Republic for so long were quickly unraveling.

This second agrarian bill became law around the same time as another piece of legislation, which gifted Caesar a five-year provincial position as governor of Gaul after his year of consul was up. The post also included several legions, fulfilling Caesar's desire for military adventurism and guaranteeing that a war would be waged in his northern province, regardless of the actual threat to Rome. Near this time, Caesar also supported perhaps the most radical policy yet: a bill which, for the first time, dispersed grain to the public completely free of charge. Bill after bill was ratified, and by the conclusion of Caesar's term as head of state, his populist agenda had been tightly woven into the fabric of Roman social life. Before Caesar left for his governorship, he cemented his association with Pompey through a wedding, marrying his teenage daughter to the forty-seven year old conqueror. Pompey was now not merely an ally, but Caesar's son-in-law.

Cato would also take leave of the city, but not willingly. An ideological fan of the Triumvirate, Publius Clodius Pulcher had devised a plan to send him away. Clodius, who was deeply invested in the populist legislative agenda, tasked Cato with clerical duty in Cyprus, which in a new foreign policy was being annexed by Caesar's administration. Officially, Cato's selection for the chore was due to his honesty, as the assignment would largely be a matter of accounting for tax collections. In reality, though, it was a way for the *populares* to free themselves of a problematic nuisance.

Seeing through the charade, Cato tried to refuse the appointment, most likely out of fear of what would happen to constitutional law in his absence, but also because, like all true republicans, he was opposed to imperial graft. After Clodius passed a bill compelling Cato's assignment, there was no legal way out. He reluctantly submitted to the law.

Much of Cato's time in Cyprus was spent tending to the assets of the late King Ptolemy, who had poisoned himself after hearing the news of Rome's intentions. Cato's nephew Brutus, who would later gain an assassin's notoriety from William Shakespeare's tragedy, accompanied his uncle to assist with the tedious bookkeeping. After settling a civil conflict in the nearby city of Byzantium, Cato set sail for Rome where, by stroke of misfortune, a fire along his return trip consumed the records he had painstakingly kept from the proceeds of the king's estate. Despite the loss of documentation from roughly two years of work, no one in Rome dared to seriously question Cato's integrity. Even his powerful enemies could not muster enough credibility to bring charges of corruption. The Stoic's word was more than enough.

Social turmoil: The swelling Warfare and Welfare State

By 56 BC, while Caesar was busy waging his Gallic conquest throughout Western Europe—periodically sending dispatches home about his magnificent victories (which Cato would forcefully condemn for his campaign's genocidal slaughter)—Pompey and Crassus declared their intentions to jointly seek another consulship. After achieving land for his veterans during Caesar's consulship, Pompey now wanted a new foreign post for himself, ultimately deciding on a return to Roman-held Spain in the West. In the other direction, Crassus sought assignment in Syria, an untapped territory that could surely reward its commander with plunder and military glory. Operating from Gaul, Caesar looked for an extension to his command to allow for more time to win battles and postpone the ability of his enemies to prosecute him on corruption charges, a frequent tactic in Roman politics after legal immunity from a proconsul's tour of duty expired.

Cato found himself in the now all-too-familiar position of leading the resistance. The Republic was fading with welfarism at home, while its shape abroad was assuming the form of an empire, divvied up for maximum loot and parceled out between the men with the most legions. The *optimates* in the Senate were still a solid force, but their ranks had been weakened over the years, picked off in one form or another by the Triumvirate's money and power. Even Cicero had cozied up to Pompey and Caesar after certain strings had been pulled to lift Clodius's banishment of the orator, a temporary exile that had come about from a personal feud (though the overt legal reasons were owed to Cicero's handling of the populist Catiline conspiracy). Nonetheless, this left Cato with a lonely job again.

The election of the two men of the Triumvirate still remaining in Rome was a forgone conclusion. To impede their agenda, Cato stood for the office of praetor, second only to the consulship. On his way to the polls, he was ambushed by a gang of thugs, most likely hired by Pompey or Crassus. His supporters fled in panic, but Cato, in spite of a knife wound to the arm, pressed onward, speaking against the two consul-elects.

After shenanigans at the ballot box, including rampant bribery and a dubious decree from Pompey postponing the vote tally in Cato's race, the Stoic lost his first election. For most Romans, the defeat would have been a blow, not only to their ego, but to their will to persist, especially after the narrow survival of an assassination attempt. But Cato, confident in purpose, forged ahead.

With Cato literally nursing his wounds, the Triumvirate easily succeeded with their plans, passing out bills allowing each of their wishes to materialize. Caesar was granted his five-year extension to rummage through Gaul, while Crassus secured his Syrian expedition. Pompey stayed behind in Rome, delegating the management of his affairs in Spain to aides. The Triumvirate exhausted a fair amount of political capital to accomplish these ends, up to and including violence, and Cato's resolve soon exploited the opening.

During the following year of 54 BC, Cato made another run at praetor, this time succeeding. Whether his victory was owed to his opponents' apathy or public backlash to their corruption cannot be known with certainty, but his win allowed him to carry on his use of the 'bully pulpit,' railing against the dangers the Triumvirate posed to the Republic. At one point, Cato made another attempt to clean up public corruption by supervising elections and proposing reforms targeting voter bribery. The blowback from this was steep, as it became evident that the public relished their fanfare of circus shows and free food, just as much as those awarding the bribes enjoyed the election results. His proposal was shot down.

Two events over the next year would drastically alter the Roman political landscape. In late summer of 54 BC, Pompey's wife Julia, Caesar's daughter, died in childbirth. Though this did not immediately weaken the bond between the two men, it did sever the family tie.

The second event of significance came in the spring of 53 BC. With some thirty-five thousand troops under his command, Crassus foolishly departed his new post in Syria to invade the Parthian Empire in the East. Marching his army through the deserts of modern-day Turkey, Crassus lacked the military mind of Caesar. On open ground, heavy but slow Roman infantry were vulnerable to a force of skilled Parthian cavalry, whose speed and mobility helped them ambush the Roman legions, inflicting severe casualties and killing most of Crassus's men. After the massacre, Crassus was lured by the Parthians to a parley, presumably to discuss terms for withdrawal, where the wealthiest man of Rome was killed. Though the relationship which remained of the First Triumvirate would survive for several more years, the changes would clearly strain the alliance between Pompey and Caesar.

In the wake of this, Rome underwent a period of turmoil. Riots and a deadlocked government were caused by a number of factors. The news of Crassus's disaster brought panic to the capital; rumors spread that the Parthians might seek revenge for his incursion, and the uncertainty from how his death would affect the balance of power was not a calming factor. Clodius, who had become quite the gangster, parading as a sort of welfare champ for the urban poor, had been killed following a street fight with a rival's gang. In the aftermath of his death, his followers turned violent in the city (at one point, setting fire to the Senate House). Throughout the melee, the *optimates* solidified their unity, and given that Pompey had already realized many of his political designs, he was more settled in the ways of a man over fifty.

As the last of the original trifecta alive and in Rome, Pompey's ties with Cato's faction in the Senate began to improve. Cato was coming to the view that of the two remaining members of the Triumvirate, Caesar was the greater threat. Unlike Pompey, who scored all of his military wins early in life, Caesar received a later start with command, and while Pompey acquainted himself with leisure, Caesar craved the life of war. With every victory he amassed, Caesar accumulated more wealth and a more experienced army, hardened from years of battle. This was a growing danger, one that had to be stopped at all costs. Even if that meant joining Pompey the Great.

With the chaos on the streets and the mindset of the looming Caesarian threat on the horizon, Cato pulled a stunning reversal in policy: he would support Pompey as sole consul. This was an unconstitutional measure, as a consul was not a king precisely because there were two elected every year. However, unable to overcome the *populares*, the government was still sharply divided, neither side gaining much in the way of advantage. Elections had been previously stalled by the *optimates* staying at home, using the absence of a quorum as a strategy to maintain the gridlock.

It was in this atmosphere that Cato saw such a move as a means to bring Pompey into the fold, which in the long run could build a coalition strong enough to take down Caesar upon his return from Gaul. In any regard, even if the lone consul should become unruly, Cato was confident Pompey could be held accountable with the help of his fellow allies. Introduced in the Senate by Bibulus, resistance to the resolution quickly dissipated with the knowledge that the former consul would take no action without his father-in-law's quiet nod. In the year 52 BC, the Senate named Pompey the solitary head of state.

Cato speaks the truth

In the midst of his military campaign, Caesar had given his support to Pompey's lone consulship, and in exchange, made a request: allow him to stand for consul from Gaul. Caesar had been carefully planning his own return. With the extension of his command set to expire in 49 BC, so too would his legal immunity. Caesar fully expected Cato and the *optimates* to prosecute him; Cato had publicly stated as much. If he could stand for consul from his province, he could deflect any such charges by slipping into another office and the full legal shield it would warrant. If not, the conqueror of the Gauls would be forced to re-enter the city as a private citizen, and most assuredly, expose himself to Cato's justice.

Pompey made good on his promise, putting forth Caesar's bill in the Senate, and as can be expected, Cato opposed the legislation with his usual tenacity. Caesar later described his view of the problematic Stoic, writing in his distinctive third-person form:

> A proposal, allowing him to stand in his absence, had been submitted…and there carried in the teeth of the violent opposition of his opponents, particularly that of Cato, who had characteristically employed his favorite trick of talking out time each day the assembly had met.

Cato's filibuster proved effective once more, skillfully using the tool to kill another deviation from traditional election law. But what was more, Pompey's proposition was intended to aid a man who was no longer seen by the Stoic as simply a populist, but as a war criminal and would-be tyrant.

It turned out, though, that Caesar's bill was not the only one on the table. Pompey approved a separate piece of legislation that passed into law, reaffirming the presence of a potential candidate within the city limits before such a person could be considered for public office. When Caesar's supporters in the Senate called Pompey on the doublespeak of his agenda, the consul played dumb. Even with reassurances from Pompey that somehow, the law would not apply to Caesar, what ensued was a lasting breakdown in trust between the consul in Rome and the proconsul in Gaul.

More than likely, the second measure was done to appease the *optimates*, but in spite of the favorable legislation, Cato took the flip-flop as weakness. Pompey had always wanted to be truly liked, and his indecisive behavior stemmed from this personality feature that became more prominent with his age. Nevertheless, the inability to determine where exactly Pompey would fall on issues of the utmost weight helped to prompt Cato's next major decision. Later that year, he would finally seek Rome's highest office, submitting his own name as a candidate for the consulship.

In what would be his last election, Cato made Caesar the defining issue. Speaking at assemblies, Cato denounced Caesar's unnecessary offensive wars, his disgraceful conduct in the name of Rome—having massacred prisoners and the innocent—and finally, that Caesar's growing power and ambition left little room for Roman *libertas*.

In spite of this alarming analysis, running on the anti-Caesar platform was challenging. The field commander had not only been busy winning battles, but winning over the public, as well. He had repeatedly made certain that exaggerated reports of his deeds in Gaul were presented to the voters, along with details of the ruthless barbarians he was supposedly keeping away from Rome. The incredible amount of loot Caesar was pouring into the capital from his conquests did not hurt his popularity either.

As a result, many Romans in the city had a favorable opinion of the proconsul.

Though Cato's style was often eccentric, as it turned out, many of his predictions were accurate. In the end, though, the crowds cared more about games and a free lunch than anything the Stoic had to say. Refusing to use bribery (or for that matter, any form of campaigning that could be construed as pandering), Cato guaranteed his own defeat in the race for the consulship of 51 BC. Yet in his mind, losing popular elections for the right reasons could be a badge of honor.

━━━━●◆●━━━━

The coming civil war

Over the next few years, the cooperative understanding between Caesar and Pompey that had built the Triumvirate disintegrated. Pompey, wishing to please everyone, became more reluctant to take clear positions in the ongoing dispute. Removed from state business in Gaul, Caesar began to interpret this hesitation as betrayal. Caesar's suspicion only increased after the widowed Pompey decided to remarry the daughter of Metellus Scipio, a long-time member of the *optimates*. To make matters worse, Pompey then named the conservative hardliner as his co-consul for the remainder of the year 52 BC.

Showing signs of insecurity, Pompey would project vast overconfidence in his power and ability. Plutarch, however, recorded that the former conqueror had fallen ill and that after his recovery, the level of public support for his health had given him a feeling of superiority:

> For while the public rejoicing was great, a spirit of arrogance came upon Pompey...he indulged himself in unlimited confidence and contempt for Caesar's power, feeling that he would need neither an armed force to oppose him nor any irksome labor of preparation, but that he would pull him down much more easily than he had raised him up.

Pompey was exceptionally dismissive when questioned over the growing tension with Caesar, making light of such a conflict, while slighting Caesar in the process. A colleague noted in a letter to Cicero that when pressed about the possibility that Caesar may choose to stand for the consulship while keeping his army, Pompey snapped back, 'What if my son should choose to strike me with his stick?' In another episode of hyperbole, Pompey responded to concerns over Caesar's intentions by bragging about his own extant influence, claiming, 'I have only to stomp my foot and legions will spring up around me.' Arrogance and naivety were helping to convert a political squabble into an armed standoff.

Several compromises were put forward to settle the escalating crisis. Since Pompey had been granted an extension to his governorship in Spain (which he had continued to manage by proxy), an idea gained steam that he should give up his province—and his control of the legions that came with it—if Caesar would reciprocate. If peace was to be had, both men should lay down their arms. Amid rumor and paranoia on each side, a flurry of offers and counteroffers proceeded, but mutually agreeable terms never came.

As Caesar saw it from Gaul, returning to Rome at the end of the year holding no office and no army would leave him defenseless against his enemies. Regardless of what might be said to the contrary, there was little practical reason to believe that anyone in Rome could hold back the legal charges Cato had pledged against him.

But this was also a convenient excuse for Caesar to indulge in his passion for power. The field general had spent almost ten years bringing a vast region under his control. His province was now nearly an empire to itself, spanning at one point, from the British isle in the north, and enveloping all of modern-day France, the German tribal areas to the east, and Italian villages in the south. Caesar accrued enormous sums of wealth from this domination—while at the same time, he perfected his military skills as a commander and shaped in battle an army that would have rivaled Alexander the Great's. In fact, not until Napoleon did an army's field commander fight in equal numbers of heavy engagements with such consistent success. Perhaps most essential for his present choice, though, even if it meant killing other Romans, this professional fighting force had become loyal to one man: Julius Caesar.

Members of the Senate crowded Pompey with various bargains to pass his former partner, conceding the consulship, or allowing a given number of legions to be maintained. Cicero tried to mediate, proposing one legion for Caesar's safekeeping, and legal immunity to boot. In what would be the final moment of failed negotiations, the Stoic convinced Pompey that appeasement was not an option: extend Caesar nothing but outright obedience to Roman constitutional law. For Cato, there could be no compromise with a tyrant.

Caesar's invasion

For Caesar, 'the die was cast.' At the turn of the year 49 BC, he marched one of his legions across the Rubicon River in northeastern Italy, a boundary enshrined in sacred law barring passage to a Roman commander with his army. On one side of this border, Caesar held lawful command; on the other, he did not. By crossing with his troops, he became an outlaw. At best, Caesar was fighting for his *dignitas*; his prestige had been insulted by the Senate, and his years of accomplishments had gone unappreciated by the establishment. More likely, Caesar resorted to war because he could no longer attain what he wanted through politics. In Cato's mind, he had to be crushed for this very reason. The only question that still lingered: was Caesar like Sulla, or Catiline?

Cato was willing to hold his nose with Pompey, just as the Stoic had done in recent years by supporting his sole consulship. Pompey was the only man in Rome seen as a match for Caesar. For starters, Pompey had experience and success leading armies in the field, beginning in northern Africa and Spain in his youth— as an ally to Sulla against the Marian factions—and again in the East against King Mithridates (after which, he was also the first Roman to conquer Jerusalem). Perhaps more importantly, Pompey had the loyalty and resources, through his wealth and personal connections, to raise his own legions—including the units already under his control in his appointed Spanish province.

With the *optimates* in the Senate, the leadership of the

republican armies had access to the state apparatus, including the public treasury and the means of conscription. Though these strengths gave ample assurance to those in the republican cause, mobilizing a large defense force from scratch would take a considerable amount of time, an element not lost on Caesar.

At Caesar's disposal were ten legions totaling forty thousand troops, a figure that his opponents would match by more than two to one. Caesar was also disadvantaged from the position of his cohorts, as his units were spread across different parts of his province prior to the outbreak of hostilities. Like the republicans, it would take time for Caesar to concentrate his forces. With the numbers against him, he opted instead for speed—and in an ancient sort of blitzkrieg, Caesar made a dash for Rome with less than five thousand soldiers.

Panic hit Rome with the news of Caesar's advance. Pompey, who had been so flippant about the prospects of 'his son with a stick,' was suddenly anything but, ordering the evacuation of the capital and eventually fleeing from Italy entirely. His hasty plan was to withdraw to Greece where he and the republicans hoped to buy time to assemble their army. As a result, Caesar's one legion captured a city of as many as half a million residents without a fight.

Several senators were assigned different provinces to manage, and Cato was charged with directing the defenses of Sicily, making his way to the island off the coast not long after Pompey's evacuation of the capital. Cato had a talent for organization, with even Caesar complimenting his enemy's skill in his memoirs on the civil war:

> In Sicily, Cato was busy repairing old men-of-
> war, and levying new ones from the various local

communities; work into which he was throwing himself with extraordinary vigor.

Caesar, having begun to consolidate his force in Rome (and confiscating much of the public treasury), sent out his own lieutenants to several of these provinces to expel their republican counterparts—a simple task at the head of their respective legions. From Sicily's hub in Syracuse, it appears Cato put up the stiffest resistance to this move, driving off Caesar's first landing party with the miniscule resources he had on hand. Soon a much larger invasion force came in its place, and with no army to speak of, chances for a proper defense were nil. To avoid throwing innocent lives away, he retired from the island and headed for Pompey's camp on the Greek peninsula.

Caesar turned his immediate attention on Pompey's proxy legions stationed to the west in Spain and, according to Suetonius, lightheartedly declared that he would be fighting 'against an army without a general, and should return from it against a general without an army.' By the fall of 49 BC, Caesar had made quick work of the resistance in Spain, though his army suffered substantial casualties from the summer's fighting. Having secured his rear, along with the rest of Italy, he set his sights to the east—on a final confrontation with his adversary in Greece.

A seaborne invasion of the Greek peninsula would require a navy, which Caesar lacked. The existing stock of merchant vessels was also insufficient for his army's transport, as Pompey had requisitioned most of the available fleet during his own escape from Italy. However, Caesar was eventually able to muster enough ships to carry roughly half his main force, which had been reduced to an estimated thirty thousand combat-ready troops after the losses in Spain. In early 48 BC, the would-be dictator launched his amphibious assault.

Cato at war

The Stoic arrived in Greece to a camp full of familiar faces. Staffed by the principal leaders of the *optimates*, Pompey's advisors had spent the previous year building the republican army. Among them were Metellus Scipio, Pompey's father-in-law and former co-consul, as well as Cato's nephew Brutus and son-in-law Bibulus, with the latter chosen to head the republican navy. Even Cicero had finally decided to take a side, joining the group after his determination that the fate of the Republic rested on Pompey's success. For better or worse, Cato had reluctantly reached this conclusion far earlier than his politically cautious friend. Within the course of only a few years, though, all of these men would be dead—and with them, the Roman Republic.

From his years of campaigning in the East, Pompey—now close to sixty years of age—had established deep connections throughout Macedonia, client states which facilitated money and soldiers to the old conqueror. Counting his Roman veterans that accompanied him to Greece, Pompey amassed an army of forty-five thousand. In addition to this sizeable infantry force, another great benefit lied with his cavalry, which totaled seven thousand and handed Pompey a seven-to-one advantage over Caesar's horsemen. Five hundred warships also guaranteed Pompey a steady flow of supplies through Dyrrhachium, a coastal port situated in modern-day Albania. The sheer numbers and logistics clearly tipped the odds in the elder general's favor.

Caesar wished to spare little time after his successful sea crossing, more than once risking the republican naval blockade to ferry his troops over the Adriatic. With long-awaited reinforcements from Marc Antony, who had proven a capable lieutenant, Caesar had with him at most twenty-five thousand legionaries. What he lacked in numbers, though, he made up in other areas, particularly experience. Unlike Pompey's army, most of Caesar's men had been with him in Gaul. These were not raw recruits. They were hardened veterans of a decade's worth of forced marches and hand-to-hand fighting, united by an unwavering faith in their younger, fifty-one-year-old commander (so tight was this bond, it was said that Caesar knew all his centurions by name). Seizing the initiative yet again, the nimble tactician who had vanquished Gaul's barbarians drove his legions straight towards Pompey.

Besides his natural inclination for action, Caesar had good reason to engage quickly. While the enemy could be restocked from its large naval fleet and seemingly endless flow of resources, Caesar had no such supply line. His legions could not last long in foreign country, and if victory was to come, he needed to provoke battle as soon as possible. Caesar sought an immediate decision.

Dug-in on a hill near his supply point at Dyrrhachium, Pompey's position had been well-fortified. Even so, his troops were green, many never having seen combat or, for that matter, service at all with the Roman army. The news of Caesar's approach brought anxiety to the republican lines, and several of the army's officers tried to curb the nerves of the troops with impassioned speeches.

Of all the pep talks Pompey had lined up, it was said that only Cato could rally the men. The soldier's soldier who had lived with his troops in the trenches all those years ago in Macedonia—a garrison not far from the very camp they now occupied—could still connect with the men in the front lines. As Plutarch described it:

> ...when Pompey himself was trying to incite his forces to a battle before Dyrrhachium, and bidding each of the other commanders to say something to inspire the men, the soldiers listened to them sluggishly and in silence; but that when Cato, after all the other speakers, had rehearsed with genuine emotion all the appropriate sentiments to be drawn from philosophy concerning freedom, virtue, death, and fame, and finally passed into an invocation of the gods as eye-witnesses of their struggle on behalf of their country, there was such a shouting and so great a stir among all the soldiers thus aroused that all the commanders were full of hope as they hastened to confront the peril.

Caesar's push towards the port was bold but ultimately ineffective. Having just beaten Pompey into position close to the supply depot, he tried for a time to lay siege to the republican army, shoveling ditches and constructing ramparts around Pompey's formation, engineering work that Caesar's troops had mastered in Gaul. The subsequent battles devolved into a form of ancient trench warfare, with both sides crossing 'no man's land' to test the strengths and weaknesses of the other.

At one point, a portion of Caesar's ranks nearly collapsed following one of several assaults exchanged between the two opposing lines. Chaos from the botched attack created panic, even for Caesar's veterans, and nearly snowballed into a fiasco for the junior field general. Caesar could hardly afford a long stalemate, much less a protracted free-for-all straining his undernourished men. His numbers were simply too small and his rival's resources too great. With Pompey comfortably equipped behind strong defenses—countering the opposition's every move through superior interior lines—Caesar broke contact and ordered a general withdrawal.

But Pompey may have been too comfortable, failing to follow up the tactical victory and missing an opportunity to finish Caesar's confused cohorts in their retreat. Aware of the disarray that could have spelled disaster for his outnumbered army, Plutarch noted a pointed remark from Caesar, which also sheds light on the appraisal he held for his cautious adversary: 'Today the enemy would have won, if they had a commander who was a winner.' For the moment, though, Caesar would have to wait to find his decision elsewhere.

Pompey's camp was overjoyed, as Caesar's march inland was the first reversal of fortune since civil war erupted. Though they suffered losses, Caesar likely received more casualties in the struggle. In their exuberance, several of the *optimates* urged Pompey to pursue Caesar and end the conflict with a final blow. Pompey never sought a decisive engagement, though. His logistical strength convinced him that attrition was the more sensible course of action, one which would allow him to rely on his abundant resources and secure supply routes to outlast Caesar's offensive. However, Pompey's indecisiveness caved to the demands impressed by his cadre.

While chase was given to Caesar, Cato was left to command the small detachment guarding the supplies at Dyrrhachium. Ostensibly this was due to Cato's gift for organization, but rumor had it that Pompey was already planning the future. After Caesar's defeat, he wished to avoid any of Cato's stubborn influence on the post-war political environment, and leaving him behind would make certain that Cato would be denied any forthcoming glory from a republican triumph. For his part, the Stoic did his duty, free of complaints.

Pompey's demise

In early August of the year 48 BC, the decisive battle finally came to a head on the plains of Pharsalus, in central Greece. Pompey's army had closed on Caesar's retreating columns, and for days, the two armies maneuvered near each other in an operational search for the upper hand. Pompey situated his troops on top of a small hill overlooking a wide field, inviting Caesar's distant forces to assault his position of strength on high ground. Suddenly, Pompey moved his men forward down the sloping ridge and out onto the open plain. Recognizing the opportunity, Caesar turned and prepped his legions for pitched battle.

Pompey devised a respectable strategy. With as many as

forty-five thousand legionaries, he stacked his troops in standard formation, several lines deep, butting his right flank up against the nearby River Enipeus. On his left, he massed his numerically-superior cavalry, over six thousand strong. With a drawn-out distance of perhaps a mile separating the two armies, Pompey had given orders for his legions to hold their position, and with his two-to-one advantage in manpower, his rested men were to absorb the weight of Caesar's tired infantry charge. Pompey's cavalry would respond with an assault on Caesar's right flank, overwhelm his opponent's smaller numbers, and take his army from the rear. It was a classic 'hammer and anvil' tactic and might well have worked had Pompey been facing Persian and Greek slaves with King Mithridates, rather than the professional Roman warriors under Julius Caesar.

Across the exposed plain, Caesar had formed his own army, which now amounted to no more than twenty-two thousand. To match the length of Pompey's lines, his smaller quantities of troops had to be arranged in a shallower depth, using the river in similar fashion to buttress his left flank. With no more than one thousand armed riders, Caesar would be severely handicapped. Yet the stationing of Pompey's horsemen, done in plain sight, telegraphed his adversary's plan, allowing Caesar to prepare accordingly. Along with his cavaliers, Caesar anchored his right flank with one of his best legions, while personally taking local command of this wing of the army where he correctly judged the main thrust of Pompey's attack to come. Thinning his lines even further, Caesar made the additional adjustment of removing more of his veterans from the regular formation and repositioned them into a reserve force on his right, taking care to conceal this relocation from the enemy's battlefield view. He even issued *ad hoc* weaponry instructions to these special units not to hurl their javelins, but to use them as spears in order to stab at the enemy horses and break up the opposition's cavalry assault. Caesar had been meticulous, and his investment in detail fetched a large return.

Within a matter of hours, it was all over. Caesar's infantry assault tied up Pompey's troops in the center, which having withstood the initial shock, maintained their formation against the seasoned veterans. As expected, Pompey's cavalry countered by slamming into Caesar's right flank, beating back his outnumbered horsemen. But in the excitement, Pompey's untested cavaliers quickly morphed into a muddled mob, and the weight of Caesar's reserve units shattered their fleeting gains, sending the entire mobile force bolting for the hills. With Pompey's cavalry routed, Caesar surged forward against his rival's exposed left wing, committing the rest of his cohorts to the attack and rolling up Pompey's flank. Panic rippled through the remaining republican line, and their entire formation started to crumble. In disbelief, Pompey watched the disaster unfold. Then he turned and ran, leaving the republican army to be cut to pieces.

It was an utterly lopsided finish—a total victory for Caesar and complete destruction for Pompey. Caesar claims to have killed fifteen thousand of the enemy, while capturing another twenty-four thousand. By comparison, Caesar's losses were miniscule, at just a few hundred. Even with the conservative figures provided by more impartial sources, the results of the battle were dramatically disproportionate. Pompey fled with his family to Egypt, where he expected to gain support from friends at court. On his arrival, he was stabbed to death by Roman officers hoping to gain favor with Caesar. In a pitiful manner, the life of Pompey the Great came to an end. Caesar was said to have wept. But gazing out over a field littered with the Roman dead, Suetonius recorded the victor's unforgiving words: 'They would have it so.'

Resist to the end

Back at Dyrrhachium, Cato received the news of the catastrophe and, in Stoic fashion, proceeded with his duty to lead in the uncertainty. He issued orders to his troops that so long as Pompey was alive, they would hold their position against Caesar. If not, he would relieve them of their posts and send them home—and then go into exile. Notwithstanding, the surviving leaders soon gravitated around Cato, the man who embodied the Republic. With still no word of Pompey's fate, Cato was committed to carrying on the resistance.

To do so, he needed to buy time—if he and the others were to have a chance at all. He set his sights on Utica, the capital city of Roman Africa. If Pompey was still alive, he had likely gone to one of the client states nearby, where he was known to have friendly financial connections. Utica would place them close to these potential allies, allowing the possibility of favorable conditions to materialize should Pompey emerge with another army. More importantly for the short term, the move would put distance between Caesar's main army and what was left of the republican resistance.

A handful of the *optimates* still in the struggle would follow. Cicero, as the senior-ranking senator left of the resistance, was offered overall command by Cato—though with the excuse of no martial abilities, the lawyer decided to part ways. Bidding Cato farewell, the orator returned to Rome frustrated and dismayed by the outcome of Pharsalus. The African-bound group also consisted of Pompey's sons, along with two commanders of the Spanish legions who had been defeated by Caesar the year before, including one Marcus Petreius—the man who had once told Caesar he would rather be in prison with Cato than share the Senate with the populist consul. Northern Africa was not prison, but for all intents and purposes, it might as well have been.

In early 47 BC, Cato and the remnants of the republicans arrived in Utica. The Stoic had led his ten thousand troops on a five hundred mile march across the barren desert, bearing the heat and the pain of the trek with the philosophical discipline he had spent a lifetime mastering. Wasting no time relaxing within the walls of the city, Cato's organizational skills proved of service once again.

Situated on the coast of the Mediterranean in present-day Tunisia, during Cato's stay over the next year, Utica would effectively serve as the provisional seat of the Roman Republic—a government now in exile. The city itself was located not far from the site of Carthage, Rome's infamous old adversary, which at the urging of Cato's own great-grandfather, had been razed to the ground by Roman armies a century before. A hub of commercial activity, Utica was a prosperous trading center, and with his efficient management of government business, Cato also made certain the native residents were fairly treated by their new Roman guests—a long-standing policy rooted in Stoicism that Cato had always encouraged.

Metellus Scipio also arrived in Utica. A one-time romantic

rival with Cato, Pompey's father-in-law had survived the battle of Pharsalus, oddly optimistic about their chances of victory in the end. Scipio was quite different from the Stoic. Descended from the great Roman general who had defeated Hannibal, Scipio lacked discipline and, at times, took credit for accomplishments that were modest at best. As governor of Syria, he had also enjoyed levying heavy taxation on his province, a practice the Stoic abhorred. According to Appian, Cato could have easily asserted his command of what was left of the Republic's army. After all, many of the troops on hand had slogged through deep sands and the scorching heat of Africa's desert following him to Utica, and given his superb competence, the remaining inner circle of the republican council looked to the Stoic for leadership. However, Scipio was a former consul, the one high office Cato had failed to attain. In spite of their past differences—which had notably involved a dispute over a wedding engagement in their youth—Scipio still outranked Cato. Demonstrating his strict adherence to constitutional law, Cato voluntarily deferred overall command to the former consul.

With insufficient means and the knowledge of Pompey's death, Cato prudently saw that the only hope for the resistance was to outlast one of Caesar's notorious sieges that was sure to come. To that end, he spent his time fortifying the city's defenses and preparing supplies. Scipio on the other hand longed to gain glory in Africa like his distant ancestor and naively held that he could prevail against Caesar's forces in open battle. Over Cato's objections to this fool's errand, Scipio would get his chance.

By 46 BC, Caesar landed in Africa. Business in Egypt had distracted him from military operations where he had spent time resolving civil conflict and internal squabbles at Egyptian court, placing his mistress Cleopatra on the throne. He had also returned to Rome to squash a mutiny among some of his legions who, starved for the pay and land promised them, demanded compensation for their past services. With these affairs in good order, he turned his attention on Cato's holdout to finish the war once and for all.

Outside the port of Thapsus, Caesar formed a daunting force of at least eight legions, around half of whom were hardened veterans. Metellus Scipio, joined by the native Numidian King Juba, annexed his troops with local manpower to produce an army that surpassed Caesar's in number but was far outmatched in both experience and the quality of leadership commanding it. As Cato had warned, the engagement was a slaughter. Caesar's ranks annihilated Scipio's force, cutting down his mixed army and massacring some ten thousand of his men—while Caesar's own legionaries took less than six hundred casualties. Scipio escaped by sea, only to kill himself soon after being overtaken by Caesarian warships.

Virtue over vice

Cato reacted to the news of Scipio's ruinous calamity with the prototypical calm demeanor expected of a forty-eight-year-old practicing Stoic. Addressing the remaining Roman republicans in Utica, he confirmed the tragedy with serene composure and, with no prospect left to resist Caesar's legions, directed the evacuation of the town.

Ruthless as he was, Caesar had long observed a policy of clemency, famously pardoning his enemies in public displays of compassion. This held utility for the dictator, helping to alleviate festering grudges that could be otherwise harbored by the friends and family of his opponents. More importantly, it was an exceptionally effective tool for propaganda. Both sides of Rome's civil war had claimed the moral high ground. While Cato was the face of the Republic's sacred constitution, mercy had always been Caesar's counter—a go-to tactic to prove his claim held the greater righteous weight. Though Caesar had been balefully wronged, he was willing to forgive.

Cato was definitely aware of the pardon the dictator was sure to extend him, just as the populist had done with several of his close associates, including his nephew Brutus and his philosophical friend Cicero. By itself, the propaganda value to the new autocrat had guaranteed such amnesty. But Cato would have none of it. After one of Caesar's relatives pleaded with the Stoic to accept the general's pardon, Plutarch noted Cato's short reply:

> I am unwilling to be under obligations to the tyrant for his illegal acts. For he acts illegally in saving, as if their master, those over whom he has no right at all to be the lord.

As Cato saw it, Caesar was a tyrant and traitor to the constitution. Tyrants possessed no ability to pardon in the first place—for by nature, despots need legal absolution themselves and cannot exonerate the crimes of others. Also, forgiveness could not be given for transgressions never committed.

Convening his supper table, Cato dined with loyal

family and friends who had stayed behind, including his two philosophers who accompanied the senator to the African town. Dinner conversation turned to philosophy, and the principles of Stoicism were debated, with Cato resolutely defending a pillar of Stoic thought that 'the good man alone is free.' He retired to his chamber, where he read Plato's dialogue *Phaedo*—a discourse covering the death of Socrates and his discussion over the immortality of the soul. After finishing the Greek text, Marcus Porcius Cato drew his sword and took his own life.

Cato's suicide was the denouement of a man who dedicated a lifetime to principle, no matter where the consequences from such a life may lead. His final act deprived Caesar a victory, with Plutarch later writing of Caesar's reaction: 'Oh Cato, I begrudge you your death, for you begrudged me the sparing of your life.' With his passing, the populist propaganda that would have been achieved through acquitting the epitome of Caesarian opposition was outright denied. Cicero would go on to publish the pamphlet *Cato*, praising his friend and his Stoic virtue defending the republican cause. Though the work did not survive the centuries, it was said to have been wildly popular within Rome. Caesar would respond in kind with his *Anti-Cato*, a piece also lost to the ages that vehemently criticized his archenemy, but ultimately bombed with its Roman audience.

Following Cato's death at Utica, the populists marched on to unimpeded power, and Caesar was proclaimed dictator for life. Not long after the Ides of March in 44 BC—the day Cato's nephew Brutus helped his conspirators assassinate the one-man ruler—the remaining republicans were wiped out through a brutal political purge. Branded enemies of the State, thousands were slaughtered, including one-third of Rome's senators.

Cicero was murdered by Marc Antony's partisans, with Caesar's faithful lieutenant brandishing the orator's decapitated head and lopped-off hands to a crowd in the Forum, before nailing the severed body parts to the Speakers' Platform. Brutus and his co-conspirator Cassius both committed suicide after their defeat in battle, but Cato's ideological followers were hunted down and executed. In many cases, even the families of these republicans were not spared.

When Caesar's nephew Octavian triumphed over Marc Antony, assuming absolute power as Augustus, the Roman Republic forever forward became a Roman Empire. In effect, the Republic had already died with Cato, for under the Caesars, populist policies only expanded. With their ever-increasing ways of welfarism and imperial wars of conquest, the Roman nation itself eventually imploded into extinction.

———◆———

Victory will be rare

Much can be learned from Cato's life. Unfortunately, he is little remembered today. Some of his forgotten memory comes from the absence of material, for the Stoic did not pen philosophy; he was too busy living it. But the bigger reason for his missing pages of history may lie with his losing cause. In spite of Lucan's famous line—'The victorious cause pleased the gods, but the vanquished cause pleased Cato'—the past is not recorded by the conquered, but by the conquerors.

Today, grade-school text books cover the usual laundry list of characters from the period: Caesar, Pompey, Cicero, Crassus, Marius, and Sulla are all typically found in the section on ancient Rome. The Stoic, though, is conspicuously absent. Even in more thorough academic studies, Cato is commonly an afterthought— an honorable mention, curtly dismissed as a minor player never making the major leagues, as if he was a speed bump on the highway toward ancient Rome's manifest destiny.

Even worse, in the advent of his rare appearance, Cato has been portrayed in pop culture as an old dimwitted crank (as he was in HBO's miniseries from 2005, *Rome*). On the contrary, all evidence suggests that he was not only exceptionally bright, but tremendously respected, even by his enemies (not to mention, years younger than his other famous contemporaries like Caesar and Cicero).

Hostility towards the Stoic can also be detected within the work of many modern historians. Several of Cato's decisions are often disparaged or even blamed for causing the civil war. Two of these cases are often the most recurring: Cato's refusal to accept Pompey's early overture for an alliance via family marriage, pushing him toward the union with Caesar, and Cato's later influence on negotiations between the two generals prior to the conflict, urging Pompey to reject Caesar's bargaining to preserve command of several legions after the expiration of the proconsul's term in Gaul.

Such criticism is little more than Monday morning quarterbacking and widely undeserved. Of the first, Cato could not foresee the formation of the First Triumvirate to begin with, as Pompey and Crassus had always been at odds ever since Pompey had stolen the latter's thunder after his victory against

Spartacus. To add to this, Cato at the time had every reason to suspect Pompey as the foremost threat to the Republic, as he had access to loyal veterans and had already demonstrated his willingness to use an army to reach his political goals (in his election for the consulship of 70 BC). Had Cato submitted to the offer, he would have very likely lost credibility with many of the *optimates*, the Stoic's base of support in the Senate, who would have good reason to question character. As Aristotle pointed out regarding such influence, 'Character may almost be called the most effective means of persuasion.'

This twenty-twenty hindsight is also entirely biased, exclusively focusing on merely one side of the choices made, particularly with the second instance. Civil war was not initiated by Cato, but by Caesar, who could have simply obeyed the constitution and relinquished his command as the law required. Furthermore, Caesar's grand adventurism and ambition for military exploits in his province was his own doing, and had he not waged such unnecessary offensive wars, any threats of charges brought against him after his governorship would likely have carried little weight. Caesar chose to commit war crimes and mass genocide— not Cato.

There is underlying rationale for Cato's fall from grace over the last century. Cato had represented virtuous purity. In recent decades, such qualities no longer characterize honor. Unfortunately, they can be synonymous with impractical foolishness or hardheaded idiocy, and more often than not, these traits are despised by the populists dominating political discourse today. In the modern era, compromise became virtue, whereas consistent principle became vice.

Another prime motive is the growing admiration for

centralized power, along with military conquest, which Cato ardently opposed. Even the study of Cicero, with all of his surviving personal letters and works in philosophy, has taken a backseat to the multitude of biographies that have come out praising Julius Caesar. Cato went to his death over his resistance to such power. Caesar denotes it, and though power destroys, it is also venerated.

During an age when nation-wide crisis was the norm, Cato's endurance through his many personal and political ordeals makes him more than a footnote. He should be realized again as the central committed figure who stood against forces which ultimately destroyed the Roman way of life. Alhough his Republic lost in the end, Cato's example went on to inspire other successful causes throughout history, including the American Revolution. And though his memory has faded, a resurgence of his life is greatly needed.

In many ways, for the present-day Stoic—especially the one underneath the statehouse—Cato is a superb model to emulate. A century after his death, this sentiment was echoed by Seneca, whose words are a testament to the life of the most principled statesman from the ancient world: 'Choose therefore Cato... picture him always to yourself as your pattern. For we must indeed have someone according to whom we may always regulate our character.'

PART III

Stoic Counsel

Applying the Classical Method of Moral Conduct

"Persist and Resist."
— *Epictetus*

Know what you can control and what you can't

"Who then is still able to hinder me contrary to my own judgment, or to compel me?" — *Epictetus*

The most important standard is understanding what you can control and what you cannot control. This knowledge is the foundation which establishes the conduct of the Stoic's personal life. Within your control are your judgments, opinions, desires, and choices. Anything outside of this internal realm is open to exterior influence and, by default, beyond your authority to direct. Turn your attention inward, where you have supreme command. If you lose this focus, you are like any other person of the multitude, deceived by the illusion you hold sway over things you do not.

As an elected legislator, one of the chief areas of concern, falling completely within your control, is how you choose to cast your own votes: Yes or No. Not only is this entirely within your control, the act of voting is your primary duty as a legislator.

This domain of your legislative life must be mastered immediately. Hundreds of bills will be presented by your colleagues and, more than likely, most will not be in agreement with the principles of liberty. Remain steadfastly consistent.

Do not become distracted by comments to the contrary. How others vote and what they say and do are outside of your concern. Many of your colleagues will give grand speeches, tailored for the masses. They will fill their rhetoric with platitudes, ripe with emotion, but devoid of reason. Ignore this propaganda.

Focus on the bill before you and whether the content conflicts with First Principles. Remember, you are in the bowels of government; one law produced after the next is its nature. Chances are, you will have to repeatedly vote No. And you may often be the lone vote of opposition. If initially apprehensive about this repetition of disapproval, imagine the worst thing that could develop from it. Mentally agree to the consequences. If you must vote No a thousand times, so be it. Nothing can force your sanction of pointless regulations or unjust laws.

Moreover, make every effort to avoid missing votes, and unless by rare circumstance it truly serves the greater cause of liberty, do not intentionally abstain from one.

Be comfortable by yourself

"If you want to improve, be content to be thought foolish and stupid."
— *Epictetus*

Realize you are alone. Alone in your beliefs. Few are inclined to agree with your positions, and of these, fewer are willing to carry them out. Quietly welcome this state of personal isolation. When this is accomplished, you can be satisfied with your own company. If not, you will desire friends, and such desire can be valued greater than your political principles.

You must forego power

"You know yourself what you are worth in your own eyes; and at what price you will sell yourself. For men sell themselves at various prices. This is why, when Florus was deliberating whether he should appear at Nero's shows, taking part in the performance himself, Agrippinus replied, 'Appear by all means.' And when Florus inquired, 'But why do not you appear?' he answered, 'Because I do not even consider the question.' For the man who has once stooped to consider such questions, and to reckon up the value of external things, is not far from forgetting what manner of man he is." — Epictetus

You will never achieve high office. Accept this fate. You will not become President, or Governor, or Senator. You will not have honors and titles thrown at your feet. In fact, most of the careerist politicians will consider you a failure. And before long, you may be thrown out of any offices you hold altogether.

You must ask yourself, do you wish to remain faithful to your principles, or become a famous, power-brokering politician? Choose one or the other because regardless of what may be said to the contrary, the two are mutually incompatible. Cato knew this all too well, selecting his integrity over the consulship. Ridding yourself now of these delusions of grandeur will help ward off corruption in the future.

Introduce your own ideas, irrespective of the result

"Now is the time to get serious about living your ideals. How long can you afford to put off who you really want to be?...Put your principles into practice—now." — *Epictetus*

—

Draft bills with your ideas, based in First Principles, even if they are unlikely to pass. Introducing your own bills will help strengthen your resolve. When your ideas are open to all, you are more apt to draw criticism. Acquaint yourself with the disapproval of others, as this is necessary to build fortitude.

For instance, if you introduce a bill to abolish income taxation, you have taken a step to diminish the power of the State. When you face votes on bills designed to do the reverse, you will find them that much easier to oppose. Otherwise, you become your own hypocrite. Regardless of legislative success, the deed of introducing your own bills helps you strengthen your convictions. Principles must be practiced, and this helps reinforce them as habit.

Others will scorn you

"Begin each day by telling yourself: Today I shall be meeting with interference, ingratitude, insolence, disloyalty, ill-will, and selfishness—all of them due to the offenders' ignorance of what is good or evil...none of those things can injure me, for nobody can implicate me in what is degrading." — Marcus Aurelius

Adherence to philosophy naturally draws ridicule. Expect hostility from your colleagues. You will be ignored and laughed at. You will be denigrated with names and accused of inflexibility or immaturity. You will be labeled a fool and become the butt of many jokes. As this happens, do not give in to anger, and do not offer a defense from insults. If you are swayed by such primitive conduct, you invite twice the disgrace—for not only have you become distressed by peripheral factors outside your control, but in doing so, you have violated your political principles.

Examine this antagonism, and you will typically find ignorance to be the cause. It is pointless to react toward ignorance, much less offer a defense from it. Knowledge stands above ignorance. Thus, the well-informed can never be threatened by the uninformed. Remember this, and you will remain internally undisturbed.

Avoid making deals

"For this end then, rather help me to be such a man, and do not ask me to do this by which I shall lose that character." — *Epictetus*

———

Be wary of entangling political gamesmanship. This long tradition of wheeling and dealing can lead toward a path of personal entrapment. Vote-swapping is usually part of this maneuvering, which often entails your implicit approval of some form of iniquity—or as it's frequently characterized, electing the lesser of two evils. Only a fool genuinely assents to such a false premise. Make it your rule of thumb never to trade votes, else you end up trading your integrity.

In various forms, you will be confronted with the temptation to seemingly achieve your aims, if only you relinquish others. You will encounter propositions from colleagues who ask for your vote for their bill, and if this request is fulfilled, they will return the favor with a vote for yours. These *quid pro quo* tactics may also come in the way of ultimatums. You may be instructed by those with greater influence over the agenda that unless you submit to certain conditions, your bills will be denied a vote altogether. These propositions will always tend to violate your convictions, otherwise there would be no need for their proposal.

Some will advise you to accept these terms for the greater good. If your bill were to pass into law, they say, it will outweigh the harm done by agreeing to support theirs. Or they may say, providing less resistance to their agenda will enable you to forward more of your own. The political world shaped by bureaucrats, pundits, and the media like to promote the false 'virtue of compromise.' People who diverge from this narrative are pigeon-holed as dense obstructionists who only wish to interrupt noble progress. But this propaganda is an underhanded attempt to redefine the very meaning of virtue, in order to limit the parameters of permissible public opinion, towards the power of the State.

In every case, it is only within your control to hold your position. External bargaining should never disrupt your purpose. Regardless of what others promise or threaten, surrendering your resistance to what you know conflicts with your convictions is the unscrupulous custom of politics. Moreover, political arrangements can give you the pretense of power over things for which you have none. Deal-making for the greater good can often inherently represent the greatest bad. Reject these utilitarian ploys, for it is precisely this behavior which has aided and abetted the decay of justice.

The greatest good is virtue, and virtue is never found in vice. Most of the time, the end goals of these endeavors never materialize, and nothing is obtained, apart from your loss of character. If you merely stand your ground, you will lose nothing, yet gain much.

Don't participate in trivial pleasures

"It is not necessary to go to the theaters often, but if there is ever a proper occasion for going, do not show yourself as being a partisan of any man except yourself, that is, desire only that to be done which is done, and for him only to gain the prize who gains the prize; for in this way, you will meet with no hindrance. But abstain entirely from shouts and laughter at any person or thing, or violent emotions. And when you come away, do not talk much about what has passed on the stage, except about that which may lead to your own improvement."
— *Epictetus*

The larger the seat of power, the more vice it attracts. The capital setting has many allures designed to wine and dine politicians, and give elected officials a false sense of importance. Extravagant receptions and gourmet food are just the tip of these distractions. Not only should you abstain from these frivolous entertainments, you should not partake in extracurricular activities beyond your official duty.

Be on guard against flattery, and when the 'cheerleaders' compliment you, do not encourage it. Remain a gentleman in your conversation, but remember that sycophantic acclaim, even sincere admiration, must remain indifferent to your inner thoughts. Very well-meaning legislators can grow accustomed to this fawning and want more of it. These feelings can slowly breed a shift in their objectives, from duty to a craving for personal adulation.

When someone tells you how much they admire your qualities, nothing more than a short 'thank you' should be in order. What will you do when the fanfare finally adds caveats to their praises? 'We love how you stood tall against so and so. Will you support our bill that puts an end to liberty?' Never indulge in flattery, for it can become the mental equivalent of bribery.

Self-restraint requires practice

"Just as plants receive nourishment for survival, not pleasure—for humans, food is the medicine of life. Therefore it is appropriate for us to eat for living, not pleasure, especially if we want to follow the wise words of Socrates, who said 'most men live to eat: I eat to live.'"
— *Musonius Rufus*

To maintain focus, keep your eating habits modest. Only eat plain food; nothing fancy. When you can, make yourself physically uncomfortable. From time to time, skip a meal, or limit the calories you consume. Uphold your composure, and shoulder the discomfort in silence. Conquering the pleasure of food is essential. Learning to govern this daily desire can help you regulate your appetite for desires in general. It is fine to enjoy a good meal, but if you can master self-control of your diet, you can sharpen your mental discipline in other categories of life.

Likewise, you should construct a variety of abnormal and intermittent routines. Wake early and impose rigid physical conditioning, or every now and then, sacrifice the luxury of a mattress by sleeping on the floor. This combination of atypical habit serves more than one purpose. Pushing your body towards a hardened state does not simply generate physical stamina, but can improve mental firmness. Drills like these can also be fitting reminders to keep the right mindset. Aches and pains, along with creature comforts, should be considered internally with indifference, since they are not good or bad in and of themselves. Reaffirming this frame of mind can assist with handling otherwise distressing externals when they arise at critical levels in the course of your life.

When minor physical unease is created at irregular times, you can purge away sneaking utopian expectations, and better prepare your ruling faculty to anticipate hardship. In a word, these personal exercises can help you remember the road ahead will seldom be smooth, which in turn, allows you to meet the arrival of life's potholes with revamped equanimity.

Practices like this should never be carelessly undertaken to the extreme. Crippling your health or causing personal injury would be absurd. But when modestly done, self-control can be refined—a virtue that must be harnessed to meet your higher duties within the statehouse.

Correctly judge your observations

"For what does the man who accepts insult do that is wrong? It is the doer of wrong who puts themselves to shame. The sensible man wouldn't go to the law, since he wouldn't even consider that he had been insulted. Besides, to be annoyed or angered about such things would be petty. Instead, easily and silently bear what has happened, since this is appropriate for those whose purpose is to be noble-minded." — Musonius Rufus

As Epictetus taught to make correct use of one's mental impressions, so too must you carefully diagnose your own perceptions. Every day at the Capitol, expect unpleasant people and events. Imagine ahead of time irate phone calls from constituents. Anticipate hostility from many of your colleagues. Presume that not only will your ideas be attacked, but your character as well.

Remember that these are irrational people who are ruled by raw emotion. Practice taking in the situation at hand, and judge anything that seems displeasing according to the rule of whether it falls within your power or beyond it. Remind yourself that these people only act in such manners because they are naive.

Negative emotion masters them, but you must be the master of negative emotion.

Epictetus emphasized that while we cannot choose our external circumstances, we can always choose how to respond to them. Therefore, closely guard your own sense of reason, and you will avoid the creeping feelings of fear, anger, and aggression. In this way, you can always retain your peace of mind and preserve sound judgment.

Resist personal ambition

"But, for your part, do not wish to be a general, or a senator, or a consul, but a free man, and there is only one way to this: care not for the things which are not in our power." — *Epictetus*

In political life, the greatest attachment the common legislator grasps at is to their own office. The reasons are many. Some desire power; they enjoy ruling over others. Some may realize there is wealth to be acquired through the political process, and graft becomes their aim. Many simply lust for fame—they crave the title they possess, which grants them public attention, and they relish this feeling of elite social status.

This desire to keep their elected station can also manifest into even larger personal ambitions, for more fame or legacy. Higher and higher office is on their minds, and many will do anything to get it—or at the very least, do whatever they believe necessary to stay in their present seat of power. This includes rationalizing their own shameful decisions, to justify the self-serving path they have chosen. Power is seductive, and in the political arena, lying and cheating become standard cultural norms. For the common politician, reelection dominates their entire existence. How pitiful is this state of affairs.

You will face great temptation to fall into this same desire and must learn quickly to overcome these corrupting influences. When you are in session underneath the Capitol dome, frequently remind yourself that everything you see and touch has been constructed from resources previously seized from the people. The aim is to continually evoke reality. The people do not serve you—you serve them. This internal exercise also reasserts First Principles, which serve your constituents best.

Furthermore, habitually imagine that you will lose your next election, and afterwards, you will return to private life, whereby everyone presently around you will forget your name and perhaps your very being. Mentally accept this possibility, and be at ease if this event were to unfold. Recognize that even the longest-serving career politicians will eventually cease to hold office—and in spite of all their years of grappling to hold power, most will have only done so by rejecting virtue. If you lose your election, it's better to do it with your integrity intact.

Ignore the chatter from others

"...and when the occasion calls, we shall say something; but about none of the common subjects, not about gladiators, nor horse races, nor about athletes, nor about eating and drinking...and especially not about men, as blaming them or praising them, or comparing them. If then you are able, bring over by your conversation the conversation of your associates to that which is proper; but if you should happen to be confined to the company of strangers, be silent."

— *Epictetus*

Most politicians, and people in general, have an addiction to gossip, and sometimes you will be at the center of it. Such conversation belongs to the mob. Refrain from associating with people who entertain themselves with such talk, and pay no attention to what others say of you.

If you do not, you will at best torment your mind with misery and, at worst, tailor your actions to please those around you. Do not wish for a good reputation, and do not try to avoid a bad one.

At the Capitol, you will be flanked by many who will praise you at times, and still many more who will relentlessly deride your every action. Flattery and verbal abuse are all external and not within your control. Do not desire or shun either category. Simply do your duty with all your might and impassively greet the opinions from others as they come. The well-advised guidance of Epictetus will always highlight this directional bearing: 'We cannot control the impressions others form about us, and the effort to do so only debases our character.'

Concentrate on your main duty

"The art of life is more like the wrestler's art than the dancer's, in respect of this, that it should stand ready and firm to meet onsets that are sudden and unexpected." — *Marcus Aurelius*

Do not go out of your way to avoid genuine friendships. In fact, the longer you stay on the right path you originally established, the more people will seek out your acquaintance. However, you must always be prepared for a fight. Within the apparatus of the State, sometimes a new situation that necessitates your devotion can arise at a moment's notice.

Never allow even the closest personal relationships to distort your judgment and confuse your true objectives. So long as you adhere to your practices, you will not be distracted when your resistance to proposed legislation is required. Besides, true friends will not take offense to your higher purpose. As Aristotle noted, 'For though we love both the truth and our friends, piety requires us to honor the truth first.'

Speak the truth

"Never does a man find himself so barred from all pursuits that there is scope for no honorable activity." — *Seneca*

⟞

Time and again, you will be called upon to lead the resistance against proposed laws that violate First Principles. This resistance can come in many forms, but oftentimes, it will necessitate your vocal opposition on the floor of the legislature. Meeting this duty will demand the exercise of many virtues.

First you need to judge the violation. The magnitude and category of what is proposed will guide your action, insofar as the initiation of war calls for a different response than new regulations over lemonade stands. Suitable judgment rests on the application of the private property ethic to the proposed law. After this, voluntary exchange, proportionality, and so on. Next, labels and names should be mentally removed whenever possible, so that judgment is never contaminated with biased preconceptions. In this way, decisions will result from the use of Aristotelian logic—and not from false assumptions unwittingly invoked by your own personal history. Careful study of classical literature will aid the former; nothing can assist the latter but strict observance of rational discipline.

After a decision is reached, press forward. Large or abnormal violations of First Principles will require your voice. Given the nature of the State, seldom will you speak in favor of legislation, for nearly all governments in our present age have become mere machines for positive law. Criticize the ideas behind the bills put forth, and not the people favoring them. The personalities in play, along with the political parties they belong, should always remain indifferent to both your judgment and your level of opposition.

Keep to the main issues at hand, but without reservation or remorse, aim a spotlight over the infractions at stake. Strong disapproval to horrid ideas must be delivered, with obstruction to their implementation should such steps be deemed proper. Repeat if necessary, regardless of how uncomfortable this may make those around you. Besides, if others desire coziness, they should withdraw their backward plans. After all, you are not culpable for these schemes; they are.

Be on guard against indulging in prideful displays of oratory. Always be mindful of the difference between defending liberty, and showcasing your knowledge of liberty. Never pander to interest groups, never engage in demagoguery, and never lead your audience to assent to a falsehood. Most importantly: do not allow fear to prevent your performance, or anger to cause it.

Speak the truth, and others will follow. If not, you have still spoken the truth. This is its own reward.

Victory will be rare

"It's not what happens to you, but how you react to it that matters."
— *Epictetus*

~

Sometimes you will win legislative battles, but more often than not, your efforts will not succeed. Accept the outcome and move on. Your goal is not the external result, but to do all that's within your own control to achieve it. Remember that you will lose many fights, but unless you mistakenly allow otherwise, you needn't suffer any losses.

Be ever mindful of history. The difficult scenarios you will find for yourself have been experienced by an untold number of men and women in the past. Recall those who gave in and those who did not. Who would you rather emulate? Wise words from James Stockdale put this in perspective:

> A properly educated leader, especially when harassed and under pressure, will know from his study of history and the classics that circumstances very much like those he is encountering have occurred from time to time on this earth since the beginning of history. He will avoid the self-

indulgent error of seeing himself in a predicament so unprecedented, so unique, as to justify his making an exception to law, custom, or morality in favor of himself.

You are never excused because of special circumstance, leaving 'no choice.' You always have a choice. If you adhere to the right one, no one can truly defeat you.

Endure the consequences

"You have power over your mind—not outside events. Realize this, and you will find strength." — *Marcus Aurelius*

———

Take care to remember that no one can sway you from your purpose, much less hurt you in the process—unless you allow it. All you must do is refuse to be swayed, and you will not be swayed. Your target must always be to focus solely on what you have power over, namely your thoughts and actions. As this skill is mastered, your effectiveness as a legislator will improve. Others may see you as a threat, especially those politicians in powerful positions. When your purpose disrupts their agenda, they will eventually retaliate.

This retaliation can take many forms. Sometimes, these actions are premeditated, in an effort to neutralize your effectiveness. But much of the time, their misguided retribution is simply emotionally-charged vengeance. Name calling is common, first in private, and then in public. You may experience 'exile,' or the exclusion from certain meetings and committees. If you have been conferred special positions in the past, such as committee chair—these will likely be taken. Or you may just be ignored.

None of these measures can harm you or your purpose. If

others ignore you or bar you from their conversations, remember that their schemes were never yours anyway. Besides, your preparation has already made you content with isolation. Beyond this, being stripped of assignments to committees, extra titles, or special positions—this is not retribution, this is a reward. Now you have no attachments, no favors owed, and no allegiances. Your attention returns to your true duty, and the only real thing under your control: your principles.

Fancy titles can make you less efficient. They often breed a fabricated notion of self-importance, along with cloudy judgment. Freed of immaterial political perks, you have increased time to dedicate towards more suitable tasks. As Epictetus instructed, 'For whichever of these things happens, it is in my control to derive advantage from it.'

Mental strength takes work

"As you are careful when you walk not to step on a nail or turn your ankle, so you should take care not to do any injury to your character at the same time." — *Epictetus*

Rational discipline must be a repetitive exercise. Like muscles, your mental resilience can atrophy in the absence of effort. Train your mind throughout the year. Practice your personal conduct so that you carry yourself in the same fashion at the statehouse as you would in your own home.

Show me a casual philosopher, and I'll show you a person who acts one way in public and another in private. Show me a part-time Stoic, and I will show you a man who will break under external pressure. Continuously improve mental fitness, and you will sustain the consistency and depth of your convictions.

Practicing morality is better than proving it

"What is the product of virtue? Certainly it is tranquility or happiness. Who then makes improvement? Is it he who has read many books of Chrysippus? But does virtue consist in having understood Chrysippus? If this is so, progress is clearly nothing else than knowing a great deal of Chrysippus. But now we admit that virtue produces one thing. We declare that approaching near to it is another thing, namely, progress or improvement." — *Epictetus*

⎯⬤

The application of First Principles matters more than conversing about them. Some of your colleagues may be capable of reciting entire books from memory—about free enterprise or political philosophy. They can dazzle others with the knowledge they regurgitate. They covet their social clubs, theorizing about theory, but when it comes time to act on anything relative to their pet discussions, they turn the other way.

While understanding the doctrine of liberty is indeed important, what is more worthwhile? Talk about the elimination of taxation or not taxing people? There is a vast difference between rambling over values and undertaking their execution.

Still, many of these individuals go pathetically further. In vain attempts to excuse the vices of their votes, they ruin their integrity. Attitudes like these are common: 'I had to vote for the bill because I need to stay in power now to promote liberty later.' Some go so far as to pervert the core ideals of liberty in clever attempts to deceive others—and even themselves—that they were acting not against liberty, but in her interest. 'You see, it's all about your perspective. We liberated them from their money.'

At least the plain power-hungry politician—who carries no such rhetoric and does not bother with the disguise—may only be misguided in purpose. In the former case, though, men who shroud themselves with the language of liberty, yet work against her implementation, incur a double shame. Do not associate with such individuals. Their company is corrosive.

Build courage

"You are unfortunate in my judgment, for you have never been unfortunate. You have passed through life with no antagonist to face you; no one will know what you were capable of, not even you yourself." — *Seneca*

⚊

Advancing the principles of liberty is not easy. Immersed at the center of the Leviathan, these ideas are inherently seen as the enemy, a threat to the State's continued social domination. You will face extreme adversity, and to confront it head on, you must overcome your fear. Stoicism offers a way of life, best equipped to accomplish this tall order.

First, become an expert on the rule of knowing what falls within your control and what lies outside it. This helps alleviate stressful emotions of anxiety. After you are firmly aware that only your thoughts and choices are truly your own, you can begin to drive out the external clutter which causes uneasiness. Recall the famous maxim from Epictetus: 'Men are disturbed, not by events, but by the view they take of them.'

Next, realize that many of the frightful scenarios people imagine for their future never transpire. And if they do, these developments are rarely as earth-shattering as what they may seem beforehand. Because people spend disproportionate amounts of time dwelling on their fears, they exaggerate the magnitude of their misery, as well as the likelihood these events will ever come to be. A self-fulfilling prophecy can begin, in which you bring about the very fears you wish to avoid, followed by your own inability to deal with them. Should you fall into the mental traps caused by fear, pause to gather your reason. Then proceed to examine each irrational thought causing this negative emotion more closely, piece by piece. There's no need to suffer, when there's nothing to suffer.

Lastly, rehearse future calamities in your mind, specifically misfortunes that give you personal apprehension. Then review ways in which you would rationally respond to such events if they ever came to pass. Not only does this prepare you for the worst that could come, but it allows you to construe ways to cope with whatever 'bad' that may actually unfold. Likewise, this negative visualization enables you to properly appraise such situations, as not being as dreadful as what you initially judged them to be.

Make these techniques routine, and you can better fortify yourself with your most powerful weapon—the only one which no one can take, your reason.

Insults are to be taken, not given

"When another blames you or hates you, or when men say anything injurious about you, approach their poor souls, penetrate within, and see what kind of men they are. You will discover that there is no reason to take any trouble that these men may have this or that opinion about you. However you must be well disposed toward them, for by nature they are friends." — *Marcus Aurelius*

⟶

Do not insult others. This is unbecoming and inconsistent with virtuous behavior. When others become irate, what purpose is served if you do as well? When you are insulted, have a sense of humor. Self-deprecation is a powerful asset, which can also help you ward off false feelings of self-importance. Be careful not to make light of others, but you can always make light of the insult itself.

Abstain from acting in anger. Some people lash out with animosity because they indulge in personal gratification from such feelings. The pleasure of hatred can rival many other desires. In keeping your reason, first you must resist impulsive actions from fleeting feelings. Then with practice, by carefully sharpening your sense perceptions, you can arrive at not generating these negative emotions to begin with.

Familiarize yourself with nonconformity

"First say to yourself what you would be; and then do what you have to do." — *Epictetus*

———

More than any other social force, crowd conformity causes people to behave in manners they would privately condemn. The repercussions from this in everyday life are miniscule. In government though, this human phenomenon has led to some of the worst atrocities in history.

You must vaccinate yourself against this political disease. Acclimate yourself to disapproval. Do not long for it, but should social exile befall you, your mind must be trained to quietly endure with equanimity. Only when you internally accept true isolation can you fully muster the strength to consistently do what must be done.

The false belief in power leads to lies. Honest convictions that impede this trend are rarely welcome. Beginning alone, you may indeed end alone. But as a steadfast adherent of truth, you will constructively produce a far greater impact than the poor souls who have willfully swallowed the deceptive *status quo*. 'Persist and resist.'

APPENDICES

Further Studies for Consideration

*"You should procure as many books as are sufficient,
but none merely for show."*
— *Seneca*

Recommended Reading on Stoicism

*"The more we value things outside our control,
the less control we have."*

— *Epictetus*

For the Newcomer

Epictetus. *Enchiridion.* Dover Publications, 2004.

Marcus Aurelius. *Meditations.* Dover Publications, 1997.

Sellars, John. *Stoicism.* University of California Press, 2006.

For the Advanced Reader

Dillon, J.T. *Musonius Rufus and Education in the Good Life:
A Model of Teaching and Living Virtue.* University Press
of America, 2004.

Epictetus. *Discourses.* Penguin Classics, 2008.

Hadot, Pierre. *The Inner Citadel: The Meditations of Marcus
Aurelius.* Harvard University Press, 1998.

Long, A.A. *Epictetus: A Stoic and Socratic Guide to Life.*
Clarendon Press, 2002.

Seneca. *Letters from a Stoic.* Penguin Books, 2004.

Suggested Reading:
Free Markets & Non-Intervention

"Beware the man of one book."
— *St. Thomas Aquinas*

For the Newcomer

Bastiat, Frederic. *The Law*. Ludwig von Mises Institute, 2007.

Denson, John V., ed. *The Costs of War: America's Pyrrhic Victories*. Transaction Publishers, 1997.

Hazlitt, Henry. *Economics in One Lesson*. Arlington House, 1979.

Mises, Ludwig von. *Bureaucracy*. Liberty Fund, 2007.

Rothbard, Murray. *The Case Against the Fed*. Ludwig von Mises Institute, 1994.

—. *What Has Government Done to Our Money? and The Case for a 100 Percent Gold Dollar*. Ludwig von Mises Institute, 2005.

For the Advanced Reader

Balko, Radley. *Rise of the Warrior Cop: The Militarization of America's Police Forces*. Public Affairs, 2013.

Bastiat, Frederic. *Economic Sophisms; and, What Is Seen and What Is Not Seen.* Liberty Fund, 2016.

Bohm-Bawerk, Eugen von. *Basic Principles of Economic Value.* Libertarian Press, 2005.

Cicero, Marcus Tullius. *On Duties.* Cornell University Press, 2016.

De Soto, Jesus Huerta. *Money, Bank Credit, and Economic Cycles.* Ludwig von Mises Institute, 2009.

DiLorenzo, Thomas. *Hamilton's Curse: How Jefferson's Arch Enemy Betrayed the American Revolution—and What It Means for Americans Today.* Crown Forum, 2009.

—. *The Real Lincoln: A New Look at Abraham Lincoln, His Agenda, and an Unnecessary War.* Prima Publishing, 2002.

Fergusson, Adam. *When Money Dies: The Nightmare of Deficit Spending, Devaluation, and Hyperinflation in Weimar Germany.* Public Affairs, 2010.

French, Douglas E. *Early Speculative Bubbles and Increases in the Supply of Money.* Ludwig von Mises Institute, 2009.

Hayek, Friedrich A. *The Fatal Conceit: The Errors of Socialism.* University of Chicago Press, 1988.

—. *Prices and Production and Other Works: F. A. Hayek on Money, the Business Cycle, and the Gold Standard.* Ludwig von Mises Institute, 2008.

—. *The Road to Serfdom*. University of Chicago Press, 2007.

Higgs, Robert. *Crisis and Leviathan: Critical Episodes in the Growth of American Government*. Oxford University Press, 1987.

—. *Depression, War, and Cold War: Challenging the Myths of Conflict and Prosperity*. Independent Institute, 2006.

Hoppe, Hans-Hermann. *Democracy, The God That Failed: The Economics and Politics of Monarchy, Democracy and Natural Order*. Transaction Publishers, 2001.

Johnson, Chalmers. *Blowback: The Costs and Consequences of American Empire*. Metropolitan, 2000.

Jouvenel, Bertrand de. *On Power: The Natural History of Its Growth*. Liberty Fund, 1993.

Menger, Carl. *Principles of Economics*. Libertarian Press, 1994.

Mises, Ludwig von. *Human Action: A Treatise on Economics*. Henry Regnery, 1966.

—. *Socialism: An Economic and Sociological Analysis*. Yale University Press, 1951.

—. *The Theory of Money and Credit*. Yale University Press, 1953.

Rothbard, Murray. *America's Great Depression*. D. Van Nostrand, 1963.

—. *The Ethics of Liberty*. Humanities Press, 1982.

——. *Man, Economy, and State with Power and Market.* Ludwig von Mises Institute, 2009.

Spencer, Herbert. *The Man versus the State.* Caxton Printers, 1940.

Spooner, Lysander. *An Essay on the Trial by Jury.* Fredonia Books, 2004.

Woods, Thomas. *The Church and the Market: A Catholic Defense of the Free Economy.* Lexington Books, 2005.

Bibliography

Classical References

Ambrose. *On the Duties of the Clergy.*

—. *On Jacob and the Happy Life.*

Appian. *The Civil Wars.*

—. *Roman History.*

Aristotle. *Metaphysics.*

—. *Nicomachean Ethics.*

—. *Organon.*

—. *Poetics.*

—. *Politics.*

—. *Rhetoric.*

Arrian. *Campaigns of Alexander.*

Augustine. *The City of God Against the Pagans.*

—. *Confessions.*

—. *On Free Choice of the Will.*

Aulus Gellius. *Attic Nights.*

Boethius. *Consolation of Philosophy.*

Caesar. *Commentaries on the Civil War.*

——. *Commentaries on the Gallic War.*

Cassius Dio. *Roman History.*

Cicero. *Brutus.*

——. *Letters to Atticus.*

——. *Letters to brother Quintus.*

——. *Letters to Brutus.*

——. *Letters to Friends.*

——. *On Academic Skepticism.*

——. *On Duties.*

——. *On Ends of Good and Evil.*

——. *On the Laws.*

——. *On the Nature of the Gods.*

——. *On the Republic.*

——. *Political Speeches.*

——. *Stoic Paradoxes.*

——. *Tusculan Disputations.*

Clement of Alexandria. *Paedagogus.*

Diogenes Laertius. *Lives and Opinions of Eminent Philosophers.*

Epictetus. *Discourses.*

—. *Enchiridion.*

Herodotus. *Histories.*

Hierocles. *Elements of Ethics, Fragments and Excerpts.*

Horace. *Odes.*

Jerome. *Against Jovinianus.*

—. *Commentary on Isaiah.*

—. *Commentary on Matthew.*

Josephus. *Antiquities of the Jews.*

—. *The Jewish War.*

Justin Martyr. *First Apology.*

Livy. *History of Rome.*

Lucan. *Pharsalia.*

Lucretius. *On the Nature of Things.*

Marcus Aurelius. *Meditations.*

Musonius Rufus. *Lectures and Fragments.*

Origen. *Against Celsus.*

—. *On First Principles.*

Orosius. *Histories Against the Pagans.*

Plato. *Phaedo.*

—. *Republic.*

Pliny the Elder. *On Natural History.*

Pliny the Younger. *Letters.*

Plutarch. *Life of Alexander.*

—. *Life of Antony.*

—. *Life of Brutus.*

—. *Life of Caesar.*

—. *Life of Cato the Elder.*

—. *Life of Cato the Younger.*

—. *Life of Cicero.*

—. *Life of Crassus.*

—. *Life of Gaius Gracchus.*

—. *Life of Lucullus.*

—. *Life of Marius.*

—. *Life of Pompey.*

—. *Life of Sulla.*

—. *Life of Tiberius Gracchus.*

—. *On Stoic Self-Contradictions.*

Polybius. *Histories.*

Sallust. *The Conspiracy of Catiline.*

—. *The Jugurthine War.*

Seneca. *Letters.*

—. *On Anger.*

—. *On the Firmness of the Wise Man.*

—. *On the Shortness of Life.*

—. *On Tranquility of Mind.*

Simplicius. *Commentary on the Enchiridion of Epictetus.*

Sophocles. *Philoctetes.*

Stobaeus. *Anthology.*

Strabo. *Geographica.*

Suetonius. *Life of Julius Caesar.*

Tacitus. *Annals.*

—. *Histories.*

Tertullian. *Apologeticus.*

—. *On the Spectacles.*

Thucydides. *History of the Peloponnesian War.*

Valerius Maximus. *Nine Books of Memorable Deeds and Sayings.*

Velleius Paterculus. *Compendium of Roman History.*

Virgil. *Aeneid.*

Xenophon. *Memorabilia.*

Modern References

Acton, John Emerich Edward Dalberg. *Lord Acton: Essays in Religion, Politics, and Morality; Selected Writings of Lord Acton.* Liberty Fund, 1988.

Adams, John. *The Revolutionary Writings of John Adams.* Liberty Fund, 2000.

Addison, Joseph. *Cato: A Tragedy in Five Acts.* Watchmaker Publishing, 2010.

Alighieri, Dante. *Divine Comedy.* Oxford University Press, 1961.

Alinsky, Saul. *Rules for Radicals: A Pragmatic Primer for Realistic Radicals.* Random House, 1971.

Anderson, Virginia DeJohn. *The Martyr and the Traitor: Nathan Hale, Moses Dunbar, and the American Revolution.* Oxford University Press, 2017.

Aquinas, Thomas. *Commentary on Aristotle's "On Sense and What Is Sensed" and "On Memory and Recollection."* The Catholic University of America Press, 2005.

——. *Commentary on Aristotle's "Posterior Analytics."* St. Augustine's Dumb Ox Books, 2008.

——. *Disputed Questions on the Virtues.* Cambridge University Press, 2005.

——. *On Kingship: To the King of Cyprus.* Pontifical Institute of Mediaeval Studies, 1949.

—. *On the Principles of Nature.* The Fig Classic Series on Medieval Theology, 2013.

—. *Summa contra Gentiles.* University of Notre Dame Press, 1975.

—. *Summa Theologica.* Benziger Brothers, 1947.

—. *Truth and the Disputed Questions on Truth.* Catholic Art Society, 1992.

Balko, Radley. *Rise of the Warrior Cop: The Militarization of America's Police Forces.* Public Affairs, 2013.

Bastiat, Frederic. *The Law.* Ludwig von Mises Institute, 2007.

Birley, Anthony. *Marcus Aurelius: A Biography.* Routledge, 1987.

Borden, Morton, ed. *The Anti-Federalist Papers.* Michigan State University Press, 1965.

Boter, Gerard. *The Encheiridion of Epictetus and its Three Christian Adaptations: Transmission and Critical Editions.* Brill, 1999.

Browning, Christopher R. *Ordinary Men: Reserve Police Battalion 101 and the Final Solution in Poland.* Harper Collins Publishers, 1992.

Brunt, P.A. *The Fall of the Roman Republic and Related Essays.* Clarendon Press, 1988.

Bryan, Mark Evans. "'Sliding into Monarchical Extravagance': Cato at Valley Forge and the Testimony of William Bradford Jr." *The William and Mary Quarterly*, 2010.

Buckley, John. *Air Power in the Age of Total War*. Indiana University Press, 1999.

Cahill, Thomas. *How the Irish Saved Civilization: The Untold Story of Ireland's Heroic Role from the Fall of Rome to the Rise of Medieval Europe*. Anchor Books, 1996.

Chesterton, G.K. *St. Thomas Aquinas*. Echo Library, 2007.

Clausewitz, Carl von. *On War*. Princeton University Press, 1989.

Copleston, F.C. *Aquinas: An Introduction to the Life and Work of the Great Medieval Thinker*. Penguin Books, 1956.

Dealy, Ross. *The Stoic Origins of Erasmus' Philosophy of Christ*. University of Toronto Press, 2017.

Descartes, Rene. *Discourse on the Method*. SMK Books, 2009.

Ellis, Albert. *Reason and Emotion in Psychotherapy*. Lyle Stuart, 1962.

Erasmus, Desiderius. *The Adages of Erasmus*. University of Toronto Press, 2001.

—. *The Complaint of Peace*. Cosimo Classics, 2004.

—. *The Education of a Christian Prince*. Cambridge University Press, 2017.

Everitt, Anthony. *Cicero: The Life and Times of Rome's Greatest Politician*. Random House, 2001.

Ferry, Luc. *A Brief History of Thought: A Philosophical Guide to Living*. Harper Perennial, 2011.

Frankl, Viktor. *Man's Search for Meaning*. Beacon Press, 2006.

Franklin, Benjamin. *The Papers of Benjamin Franklin*. Yale University Press, 1961.

Freedman, Russell. *Washington at Valley Forge*. Holiday House, 2008.

Fuller, Randall. "Theaters of the American Revolution: The Valley Forge Cato and the Meschianza in Their Transcultural Contexts." *Early American Literature*, 1999.

Furuya, Hiroyuki. "Beauty as Independence: Stoic Philosophy and Adam Smith." *The Kyoto Economic Review*, 2011.

Gibbon, Edward. *The History of the Decline and Fall of the Roman Empire*. Cosimo Classics, 2008.

Gilson, Etienne. *The Gilson Lectures on Thomas Aquinas*. Pontifical Institute of Mediaeval Studies, 2008.

Goar, Robert J. *The Legend of Cato Uticensis from the First Century BC to the Fifth Century AD, with an Appendix on Dante and Cato*. Latomus, 1987.

Goldsworthy, Adrian. *Caesar: Life of a Colossus*. Yale University Press, 2006.

Goodman, Rob, and Jimmy Soni. *Rome's Last Citizen: The Life and Legacy of Cato, Mortal Enemy of Caesar*. St. Martin's Press, 2012.

Grotius, Hugo. *On the Law of War and Peace*. Cambridge University Press, 2012.

Hadot, Pierre. *The Inner Citadel: The Meditations of Marcus Aurelius*. Harvard University Press, 1998.

—. *Philosophy as a Way of Life: Spiritual Exercises from Socrates to Foucault*. Wiley-Blackwell, 1995.

Hale, Nathan. *Nathan Hale Collection*: "Letter from Betsy Hallam, October 29, 1775." Beinecke Library, 1775.

Hayek, Friedrich A. *The Fatal Conceit: The Errors of Socialism*. University of Chicago Press, 1988.

Henry, Patrick. *Patrick Henry in His Speeches and Writings and in the Words of His Contemporaries*. Warwick House Publishing, 2007.

Herman, Arthur. *The Cave and the Light: Plato versus Aristotle, and the Struggle for the Soul of Western Civilization*. Random House, 2013.

Hoppe, Hans-Hermann. *The Economics and Ethics of Private Property: Studies in Political Economy and Philosophy*. Ludwig von Mises Institute, 2007.

Houser, R.E., ed. *The Cardinal Virtues: Aquinas, Albert, and Philip the Chancellor*. Pontifical Institute of Mediaeval Studies, 2004.

Hughes-Hallett, Lucy. *Heroes: Traitors, Bandits, Saviours and Supermen*. Fourth Estate, 2004.

Irvine, William. *A Guide to the Good Life: The Ancient Art of Stoic Joy*. Oxford University Press, 2009.

Jefferson, Thomas. "Jefferson's inscribed Flyleaves from Cicero's *De Re Publica*." The Thomas Jefferson Papers at the Library of Congress, 1823.

—. *The Writings of Thomas Jefferson*. The Thomas Jefferson Memorial Association, 1903.

Kant, Immanuel. *Groundwork of the Metaphysics of Morals*. Simon and Schuster, 2013.

Keegan, John. *A History of Warfare*. Vintage Books, 1993.

—. *The Mask of Command*. Penguin Books, 1988.

Ketcham, Ralph, ed. *The Anti-Federalist Papers; and, The Constitutional Convention Debates (with Cato V and Cato VII)*. Signet Classic, 2003.

Lebell, Sharon. *The Art of Living: The Classical Manual on Virtue, Happiness, and Effectiveness*. Harper One, 1995.

Lipsius, Justus. *On Constancy*. University of Exeter Press, 2006.

Locke, John. *Two Treatises on Government*. Cambridge University Press, 1988.

—. *The Works of John Locke: Mr. Locke's Reply to the Right Reverend the Lord Bishop of Worcester's Answer to his Second Letter*. Scientia Verlag Aalen, 1963.

Long, A.A. *Epictetus: A Stoic and Socratic Guide to Life*. Clarendon Press, 2002.

—. *From Epicurus to Epictetus: Studies in Hellenistic and Roman Philosophy*. Oxford University Press, 2006.

——. *Stoic Studies*. Cambridge University Press, 1996.

Machiavelli, Niccolo. *Discourses on Livy*. Oxford University Press, 2003.

——. *The Prince*. Cambridge University Press, 1988.

Madison, James. *The Papers of James Madison*. Read Books, 2009.

Mayor, Adrienne. *The Poison King: The Life and Legend of Mithradates, Rome's Deadliest Enemy*. Princeton University Press, 2011.

McCullough, David. *1776*. Simon and Schuster, 2005.

McLynn, Frank. *Marcus Aurelius: A Life*. Da Capo Press, 2009.

McNab, Chris. *The Roman Army: The Greatest War Machine of the Ancient World*. Osprey Publishing, 2010.

Mises, Ludwig von. *Omnipotent Government: The Rise of the Total State and Total War*. Arlington House, 1969.

Montaigne, Michel de. *The Complete Essays*. Penguin Classics, 1993.

Montesquieu, Charles-Louis de Secondat. *The Spirt of the Laws*. Cambridge University Press, 1989.

Nock, Albert Jay. *Jefferson*. Harcourt, Brace and Company, 1926.

——. *The Theory of Education in the United States*. Harcourt, Brace and Company, 1932.

Oestreich, Gerhard. *Neostoicism and the Early Modern State*. Cambridge University Press, 1982.

Paine, Thomas. *Rights of Man, Common Sense, and Other Political Writings*. Oxford University Press, 1995.

Paul, Ron. *End the Fed*. Grand Central Publishing, 2009.

——. *Liberty Defined: 50 Essential Issues That Affect Our Freedom*. Grand Central Publishing, 2011.

——. *The Revolution: A Manifesto*. Grand Central Publishing, 2008.

——. *Swords into Plowshares: A Life in Wartime and a Future of Peace and Prosperity*. Ron Paul Institute for Peace and Prosperity, 2015.

Phelps, M. William. *Nathan Hale: The Life and Death of America's First Spy*. University Press of New England, 2015.

Powell, Jim. *The Triumph of Liberty: A 2,000-Year History, Told Through the Lives of Freedom's Greatest Champions*. Free Press, 2000.

Rasimus, Tuomas, et al. *Stoicism in Early Christianity*. Hendrickson Publishers, 2010.

Richard, Carl J. *The Founders and the Classics: Greece, Rome, and the American Enlightenment*. Harvard University Press, 1994.

——. *Greeks and Romans Bearing Gifts: How the Ancients Inspired the Founding Fathers*. Rowman and Littlefield, 2008.

Robertson, Donald. *Stoicism and the Art of Happiness*. McGraw-Hill, 2013.

Romm, James. *Dying Every Day: Seneca at the Court of Nero*. Knopf, 2014.

Rothbard, Murray. *An Austrian Perspective on the History of Economic Thought*. Edward Elgar Publishing, 1995.

Seager, Robin. *Pompey the Great: A Political Biography*. Blackwell Publishing, 1979.

Sellars, John, ed. *The Routledge Handbook of the Stoic Tradition*. Routledge, 2015.

——. *Stoicism*. University of California Press, 2006.

Shakespeare, William. *The Tragedy of Hamlet, Prince of Denmark*. Hackett Publishing, 2015.

——. *The Tragedy of Julius Caesar*. Yale University Press, 1957.

Shalev, Eran. *Rome Reborn on Western Shores: Historical Imagination and the Creation of the American Republic*. University of Virginia Press, 2009.

Shields, John C. *The American Aeneas: Classical Origins of the American Self*. University of Tennessee Press, 2001.

Smith, Adam. *An Inquiry into the Nature and Causes of the Wealth of Nations*. Hackett Publishing, 1993.

——. *The Theory of Moral Sentiments*. Cambridge University Press, 2002.

Smith, George H. *The System of Liberty: Themes in the History of Classical Liberalism.* Cambridge University Press, 2013.

Stem, Rex. "The First Eloquent Stoic: Cicero on Cato the Younger." *The Classical Journal*: The Classical Association of the Middle West and South, 2005.

Stockdale, James. *Courage Under Fire: Testing Epictetus's Doctrines in a Laboratory of Human Behavior.* Hoover Institution Press, 1993.

—. *Thoughts of a Philosophical Fighter Pilot.* Hoover Institution Press, 1995.

Strange, Steven K., and Jack Zupko, eds. *Stoicism: Traditions and Transformations.* Cambridge University Press, 2004.

Strauss, Leo. *Xenophon's Socrates.* Cornell University Press, 1972.

Suarez, Francisco. *Selections from Three Works of Francisco Suarez.* Clarendon Press, 1944.

Torrell, Jean-Pierre. *Saint Thomas Aquinas: The Person and His Work.* The Catholic University of America Press, 1996.

Trenchard, John and Thomas Gordon. *Cato's Letters or Essays on Liberty, Civil and Religious, and Other Important Subjects.* Liberty Fund, 1995.

Tuchman, Barbara W. *The Guns of August.* Macmillan, 1962.

Vander-Waerdt, Paul A., ed. *The Socratic Movement.* Cornell University Press, 1994.

Vogt, Katja Maria. *Law, Reason, and the Cosmic City: Political Philosophy in the Early Stoa*. Oxford University Press, 2008.

Wapshott, Nicholas. *Keynes Hayek: The Clash that Defined Modern Economics*. W.W. Norton and Company, 2012.

Washington, George. *The Writings of George Washington from the Original Manuscript Sources*. Greenwood Press, 1970.

West, E.G. *Education and the State: A Study in Political Economy*. Liberty Fund, 1994.

Wills, Garry. *Cincinnatus: George Washington and the Enlightenment*. Doubleday, 1984.

Wilson, Emily. *The Greatest Empire: A Life of Seneca*. Oxford University Press, 2014.

Younkins, Edward W. *Champions of a Free Society: Ideas of Capitalism's Philosophers and Economists*. Lexington Books, 2008.

About the Author

Pat McGeehan is a three-term state representative in the West Virginia Legislature. A prolific writer and guest speaker, Pat has published numerous essays on economics, history, and philosophy. As a former business owner, he now helps manage a private school which caters to troubled children. Pat has also served as a military intelligence officer, and is a graduate of the US Air Force Academy in Colorado Springs. He is the author of *Printing Our Way to Poverty: The Consequences of American Inflation.* He is also the co-author of *The Liberty Essays: Restoring a Lost American Principle.* Pat resides with his daughter Kennedy in Chester, West Virginia.

CPSIA information can be obtained
at www.ICGtesting.com
Printed in the USA
FSOW03n2202240118
43771FS

9 780990 738619